TARGETS

TARGETS

How to
Set Goals for Yourself
and Reach Them!

LEON TEC, M.D.

HARPER & ROW, PUBLISHERS, NEW YORK

Cambridge · Hagerstown · Philadelphia · San Francisco
London · Mexico City · São Paulo · Sydney

Portions of this work originally appeared in *Family Circle*.

FIRST EDITION

Designer: Trish Parcell

Library of Congress Cataloging in Publication Data

Tec, Leon.
  Targets.

  1. Performance.   2. Goal (Psychology)
3. Success. I. Title.
BF503.T43   1980   158′.1   78-20190
ISBN 0-06-014241-3

---

80 81 82 83 84 10 9 8 7 6 5 4 3 2 1

To Nechama, Leora and Roland, who contribute
to my inspiration and enthusiasm

Contents

Introduction

The concepts and techniques discussed throughout this book
have evolved, in large part, out of my attempts in my practice
to give my patients practical tools with which to combat the
all-too-common problems of depression, anxiety, and low
self-esteem. It was my conviction when I began working on
this book, and it is an even stronger conviction today, that
many of the "psychological" problems that affect so many
people today have their roots in what I consider a largely
technical inability to deal effectively with some of the basic
challenges of daily living—in particular, the ability to establish and reach goals.

I am indebted to a number of people, without whose help
this book could not have been written. I want, first of all, to
thank Barry Tarshis, who worked closely with me in organizing and editing my ideas. I'm also indebted to Nach Waxman,
without whose patience and guidance the book might have
lacked some of the ingredients that will make it useful to people. And, finally, I owe a special "thank you" to Selma Weitz,
who brought to the herculean job of converting an often-
corrected final draft into a finished manuscript many of the
admirable skills I talk about throughout the book.

L.T.

CHAPTER 1

Noticing an Elephant

There's an old Russian story about a man who goes to the zoo one day and becomes so preoccupied with the butterflies fluttering around that he never notices the zoo's main attraction—a rare old elephant. I mention this story because it illustrates a problem many people have when it comes to accomplishing the things they would like to accomplish in their lives. At the root of this problem is a skill that virtually everybody has but most people fail to use to its full potential. Why? Because they don't realize the skill is there to be used. They simply don't notice it.

The skill I'm talking about—this elephant that many of us fail to notice in our lives—is something I call the ability to target—or, targeting.

Targeting is easy enough to define. It is the ability to direct behavior to recognized, predetermined objectives. This ability is related—but distinct from—the process we normally refer to as establishing goals. And it is related—yet distinct from—the process we go through when we pursue these goals.

Targeting is the means through which these two distinct processes—establishing goals and pursuing goals—are unified into one effective behavioral strategy. You can think of it as a process that organizes behavior in a way that enables you to get the most out of yourself, regardless of what your objectives are and regardless of what your skills and talents may be.

If the process I'm talking about here isn't entirely clear to you, it's probably because you take this ability for granted. You're under the impression, perhaps, that if you know what you want to accomplish and you have the skills to reach this objective, the situation will pretty much take care of itself.

But frequently the situation doesn't take care of itself. After all, most of us have been setting goals for ourselves ever since we were in school. And in most instances we are not lacking the resources to reach these goals. We want to advance in our careers, do better in school, improve our relations with other people, become more effective parents, acquire new skills, stop smoking, and lose weight—not to mention the day-to-day goals we set for ourselves: our intentions to answer letters, do household chores, get in touch with friends.

Yet, for any number of reasons, we do not accomplish these goals; we don't advance in our careers, while fellow workers who don't work as hard as we do pass us by. We don't lose the weight we want to lose. We don't improve our relationships with our children. What's more, all those little day-to-day objectives and goals manage somehow to get overlooked, too.

Not that we don't have explanations.

"I'm lazy," a person will say. "I'm disorganized. I'm not a disciplined person."

Or else a person will explain his inability to achieve objectives by describing himself (or herself) as a procrastinator, as if procrastination were something you were born with, like blue eyes or blond hair.

I don't go along with these explanations.

In my view, the reason many people have trouble achieving the objectives they hope to achieve in their lives isn't a matter of laziness, lack of discipline, disorganization or procrastination per se. And it isn't usually related, either, to the ability a person has to achieve his or her goals.

What's missing is the ability to target: the ability to organize our actions, time, and mental energies toward specific

goals and objectives. And, as I said earlier, this is an ability
we all have. More importantly, it's an ability that can be developed and improved upon without, in most cases, requiring
any drastic changes in personality and life-style.

Getting Sidetracked

Imagine for a moment that you are sitting home one evening
balancing your checkbook. Suddenly the felt-tip pen you're
using runs out of ink. What do you do? Obviously, you stop
what you're doing long enough to find something else to write
with and you go on with balancing the checkbook.

As simple and routine as the situation I've just described
may seem, it illustrates aspects of the very process we are going to be concerned with throughout this book. Balancing the
checkbook is an objective, a target you set for yourself. Running out of ink presents an obstacle to that objective. So, you
do what is necessary to deal with the obstacle, and then resume the activity that moves you closer to your objective.

Clearly, in a situation as routine and as easily solved as this
one, you're not consciously aware of an actual mental process
taking place. You don't say to yourself, "Well, now, even
though my pen has run out of ink, I'm going to allow this fact
to take my mind off my principal objective, which is to balance my checkbook." You simply do what has to be done in
the simplest way possible. Maybe you take another pen from
your pen receptacle. Maybe you go into another room to get
another pen.

No matter. The point is that you deal with a situation by
recognizing what has to be done and by taking the necessary
steps.

But now let's change the script a little bit.

We'll start it the same way, with you at your desk balancing your checkbook, and with the pen you're using running
out of ink. This time, though, instead of reaching for a new
pen, you see what you can do about coaxing additional ink

out of the one you've been using. You take it apart. You tap it against the desk. You light a match and put the flame to the tip. Or maybe you get angry at the pen and at the manufacturer who produced it, or at the stationery store who sold it to you. You call the store to complain, and maybe get into an argument with the storekeeper.

In the meanwhile, one thing is certain: Your checkbook doesn't get balanced. Dealing with the obstacle in an inefficient and inappropriate manner has interfered with the overall process of reaching the primary objective. If someone were to ask you, "Is it more important at this moment to take care of the pen or to balance your checkbook?" the answer would be clear: The checkbook takes precedence. Yet, despite this awareness and despite the availability of alternate writing instruments, you still allow yourself to get off the track you were on prior to the pen running out of ink.

The particulars of the situation I've just described to you may seem exaggerated, but the dynamics are found in many of the situations we deal with on a day-to-day basis. None of us is immune to this syndrome. Some of us are more susceptible to it than others. The situations I refer to are those in which your objective is fairly obvious but your behavior lacks focus and direction. These are situations in which you know what you want to do but nonetheless get "blocked" or "sidetracked" and sometimes do things that actually work against the possibility of achieving the objectives you set out to reach.

Some examples:

- You have a phone call to make or a letter to write that may have an important bearing on your career. You have the time to do it, but for some reason days pass and you keep putting it off.

- You have an unusually heavy workload in front of you on a particular morning in the office. Instead of getting started on it you fritter away an hour shuffling papers, making phone calls, sharpening pencils, and refilling your coffee cup.

- You decide you must have a talk with one of your children about his or her school grades. Within a minute or two, however, you are arguing about something entirely different—the way he or she takes care of his room, or why he/she got in so late last Saturday night.

- You're running a half-hour late for a dinner engagement, yet you find yourself immersed in an inconsequential television show.

Notice that in each of these illustrations, the ability to do something is not the issue. Nothing tangible, no real obstruction prevents you from making an important call or writing an important letter. You have the physical ability to accomplish each task. Nothing external or beyond your physical control prevents you from plunging into the massive workload that lies before you that morning in the office. Nothing extraordinary happens that somehow converts a discussion with your child about grades into an argument about housekeeping. Nothing interferes with the accomplishment of all these aims except your failure or inability to utilize the mental process that unites behavior with objectives.

But there's nothing to be ashamed of. We all suffer to some extent from the inability to link behavior to objectives. We're not machines. We can't be expected to perform at top efficiency at all times, or never to allow our emotions or our idiosyncrasies to sidetrack us from our objectives. Indeed, as we'll see later, people who are overly machinelike in their approach to life often fall as short of their objectives as people who are totally undisciplined.

So, in moderation, the behavioral patterns mentioned above—getting sidetracked, procrastinating, etc.—will not drastically affect your ability to achieve your objectives or to live a satisfying life. But when these patterns become a too-dominant theme in your life—when you are constantly putting off important tasks, when you constantly find it difficult to get started on big jobs, when you constantly go into a situation with one objective in mind but somehow end up pursuing another objective, when you constantly and consistently fail to notice the elephant, then, I think, it's time to take a good hard look at yourself.

And for a very good reason—in fact, the best. For in order to derive from life the satisfactions and the rewards we all want, we must be able to deal with the variety of situations that make up our lives in a way that is not only effective but that produces a minimum of stress. To underutilize the mental process that I call targeting is to squander energy, to increase greatly the likelihood of the failures, the frustrations, and the disappointments that inevitably lead to an erosion of confidence and self-esteem. Self-esteem, remember, is built on accomplishment, on the ability to solve problems and to accomplish what we set out to accomplish. Without a sense of accomplishment, without the feeling that we can be effective in our behavior, genuine self-confidence and genuine self-esteem is all but impossible. And without confidence and self-esteem, our capacity to derive joy and satisfaction from the life process itself is all but crippled.

How Targeting Can Help You Get More Out of Life

A basic aim of this book is to help you incorporate the techniques of targeting into your everyday life. Doing so will, I think, reduce the incidence of those actions that ultimately cause you to fritter away your energy, waste your time, and leave you feeling guilty about yourself. Targeting will help you to better deal with (and in some cases eliminate) the obstacles that may now be interfering with your capacity to enjoy life to its fullest—those obstacles, that is, that have nothing to do with your abilities and intelligence but have everything to do with how you use these abilities and intelligence.

But let me emphasize that when I talk about developing a more target-oriented approach to life, I'm not advocating a rigid by-the-numbers approach to life. Being target-directed does not mean being a prisoner to routine or a slave to endless lists. It doesn't mean selling your soul to a timetable. It doesn't mean living a life that is empty of spontaneity and surprise.

To the contrary, the ultimate reward of a target-directed life is that it actually frees you from being a slave to the conditions that affect you. But targeting is not a miracle drug. It's a skill—a practical skill that can help give you more control over your life, regardless of what your goals and objectives in life may be.

Let me dwell for a moment on this last point. The ideas and the techniques I'm going to be talking about are not keyed to specific areas of your life. I cannot tell you how to become a millionaire, a great tennis player, or a great lover. But what I can do is help you organize your behavior in a way that will help you reach whatever goals you have set for yourself.

It goes without saying, of course, that not everybody will find this book equally useful. There are some people—I know several and I'm sure you do, too—who seem to be naturally target-directed, who show a consistent ability to get things done with relative ease and minimal stress, who always manage somehow to push the right buttons at the right time, who are organized (but not compulsively so) and who are usually at their best in crisis situations. These are people who seem to get the most out of their resources, who seem able to control their behavior in ways that most efficiently allow them to accomplish their aims.

Such people are fortunate. We can compare them in some

ways to natural athletes, or to those actors and actresses who seem to have been born with skills that other actors and actresses must spend years trying to perfect. Concentration on the goal is one element of their success, but the question remains, how is it they are so free to concentrate? How is it they manage to avoid the distractions that so often deflect the rest of us from our targets?

Exactly how much improvement you personally can expect to get from this book is, of course, difficult to predict. But it might be useful to get some idea of how target-oriented a person you are at this very moment. I've put together some questions that are designed to measure your targeting ability. In taking the test, select the answer that, in your judgment, best describes your behavior in each of the situations mentioned. An explanation of the scoring and its implications follows the test.

1. Whenever I am faced with some small task that needs to be attended to, I attend to it right away. (a) Nearly always; (b) most of the time; (c) sometimes; (d) hardly ever.
2. Whenever I am about to go into a situation that is important to me, I take a few minutes to clarify my objectives. (a) Nearly always; (b) most of the time; (c) sometimes; (d) hardly ever.
3. Often when I am involved with a project that I know I am fully capable of handling, I get "bogged down" with inconsequential details. (a) Hardly ever; (b) sometimes; (c) most of the time; (d) nearly always.
4. I say things that I regret afterward. (a) Hardly ever; (b) sometimes; (c) most of the time; (d) nearly always.
5. When I write down a list of things to do on a given day, I manage to get everything finished that I've written down. (a) Nearly always; (b) most of the time; (c) sometimes; (d) hardly ever.
6. If I am involved in a large-scale project, I can accurately project when it will be completed. (a) Nearly always; (b) most of the time; (c) sometimes; (d) hardly ever.
7. When I am under a lot of pressure, it is easy for me to plan my day in a logical manner. (a) Nearly always; (b) most of the time; (c) sometimes; (d) hardly ever.
8. When I am faced with a number of responsibilities, I feel a

sense of being overwhelmed. (a) Hardly ever; (b) sometimes; (c) most of the time; (d) nearly always.

9. Give me a deadline and I'll meet it without trouble. (a) Nearly always; (b) most of the time; (c) sometimes; (d) hardly ever.
10. When I have a lot of things to do, I have trouble getting started on any of them. (a) Hardly ever; (b) sometimes; (c) most of the time; (d) nearly always.

HOW TO RATE YOUR TARGETING ABILITY

To tally your score on the above test, give yourself 4 points for every (a) answer, 3 points for every (b) answer, 2 points for every (c) answer, and 1 point for every (d) answer. Here's an analysis of the score.

35 to 40. If you scored between 35 and 40 on this test, you are without question an extremely target-oriented person and are highly organized in your behavior. If you also consider yourself reasonably content and a fulfilled person, there is no reason I can think of why you should read this book. It's possible, however, that you are target-directed to a negative extreme—a condition I call target-obsessed, in which case I direct your attention to Chapter 8.

25 to 34. A score in this area indicates an above-average ability to target behavior toward recognized objectives. It's likely, however, that your ability to manage your behavior efficiently varies according to the situation or activity you're involved with. This book can help you incorporate better behavioral efficiency into *all areas* of your life.

15 to 24. If you scored within this range, you are probably in the national average when it comes to target-directed behavior. Chances are you are far more target-oriented in some areas of your life than in others. By making you more aware of how targeting works and how you are already using it in some situations, the book should help you utilize this skill more effectively in all the various areas of your life.

14 or below. A score of 14 or below is a fairly reliable sign that you are not at all organized or target-directed in your behavior, which is to say that you are not coming close to realizing your behavioral potential. There is an elephant in your life, but you are consistently ignoring it.

Setting Your Own Targets

As you may have gathered by now, targeting is a mental process that all of us are capable of utilizing, yet some of us are more effective at utilizing it than others. The specific elements of this process which we'll be looking into shortly are easy enough to recognize: It's a matter of knowing what has to be done, of knowing how to do it, and of combining the two. Thus, it's a three-pronged tool. My own target in this book is to make you aware of how this tool can work better for you and to show you the techniques that can help you use it more effectively. *How* you choose to apply this process of targeting to your own life is, of course, entirely up to you.

One word of caution: Targeting in and of itself is not enough to assure success in those areas of your life where you have some preestablished goals and objectives. Objectives not realistically keyed to available resources and abilities are unlikely to be achieved, no matter how target-directed you are in your actions. While targeting is a useful tool in organizing resources to achieve certain specific goals, targeting itself can never substitute for knowledge and/or ability. On the other hand, as you ought to appreciate by now, targeting provides that additional dimension in organizing behavior that can often mean the difference between success and failure. As we go along you will see that there are different aspects to this process, and certain aspects may apply more to you than they do to another reader. My suggestion, then, is to keep your own needs and characteristics constantly in mind as you read through the book. As early as you can, try to isolate those areas of your life where you think the techniques and ideas in this book can most help you. Above all, don't be timid about experimenting with these techniques.

Remember this: Targeting, in the end, is nothing more than managing the one factor that more than anything else determines the nature of your life experience: *yourself.*

TARGET PRACTICE 1

The Importance of Writing Things Down

One of the chief purposes of this book is to help you become more "organized." Not to become a machine, but to become more orderly in your daily activities.

A good place to start is to get into the habit of writing things down—regardless of how good a memory you may think you have. Writing things down helps to keep your mind free of clutter. It makes you better able to address yourself to immediate circumstances as they come along.

If you don't already use one, buy yourself a looseleaf notebook—at least 5" x 8". Keep it in a visible and easily accessible place—on the kitchen counter, for instance, or on the night table next to your bed. In this notebook should go all the little notes you may now be writing to yourself on scraps of paper, matchbook covers, or backs of magazines. You don't need an elaborate system. Any time something comes up that requires future attention, simply write it on the next available line. Don't worry about grouping various tasks into specific categories. Don't worry, at this stage at least, about priorities. Simply get into the habit of recording *all* your potential targeting data in one central place.

For example, a page in your notebook might read as follows:

- Take blue dress to cleaners.
- Buy Mother's Day gift.
- Firm up arrangements for Saturday night.
- Get tires checked on car.
- Look into dance class for Linda.
- Watch "Masterpiece Theater" on Wednesday night.
- Get information for possible Mexican trip.

- **Make dentist appointment for Jerry.**
- **See about yoga class.**

Not all of the above notes relate to any *one* area of your life. Collectively, though, they represent a large part of what you do day in and day out in a typical week, so that each of them, in its own way, is a target. If you're like most active people, you may have as many as twenty or so targets like those above that have to be attended to within a period of two or three weeks.

Get into the habit of checking over the list first thing in the morning—maybe while you're having breakfast. Cross out targets you've reached. Use the techniques of "target sequencing" we'll be talking about in Chapter 3. At the end of the day, go back to the list to see which targets you've completed, which targets remain, and which targets have to be added.

After a week or so, you'll probably want to devote about fifteen minutes a day to consolidating the list, setting up a new page for targets that still remain to be reached.

CHAPTER 2

Developing Your
Target Awareness

Is this a familiar scene to you? It is 11:30 on a Saturday night. You're on your way home from one of the most enjoyable dinner parties you've ever attended. You turn to your spouse and you say, "You know, it was such a nice evening, we really should write a nice thank you note, or maybe even send a gift." Your spouse agrees. A thank you note, perhaps even a small gift, would be a fine gesture considering the way your hosts knocked themselves out for the party.

And it certainly would be, except for one problem. The note never gets written, a gift never gets sent. Sunday comes and goes, and so does Monday. Tuesday morning, in the middle of a meeting at work, or on your way to the supermarket, you suddenly remember what you neglected to do yesterday and the day before, and you resolve to send the note that evening. But somehow you get distracted—that evening you go out to a movie. Or friends stop by.

Before you know it, a week has passed. By now, the writing of the note no longer seems so important. It's probably too late, you think. The next time they invite us, you promise yourself, we'll bring a small gift. Maybe.

Which raises the questions:

Why do the simplest of tasks often go undone?

Why do notes go unwritten, gifts go unsent?

Why do so many of us so frequently have so much trouble doing things we want to do, and are fully capable of doing?

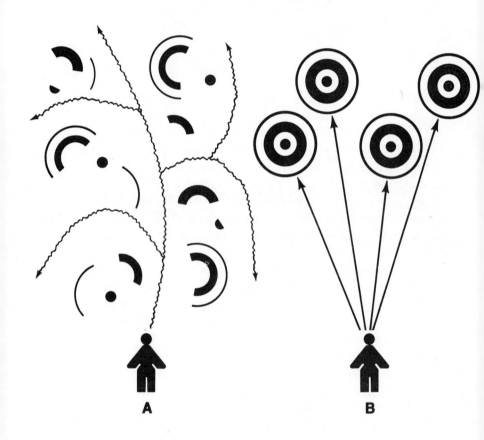

Target awareness gives shape to goals that are vague and hazy (*A*). Such goals—little more than wishes—must be structured into discrete, meaningful targets (*B*). Such an approach helps transform lack of direction into solid purpose and a plan for action.

The easiest way to explain why we sometimes have trouble getting around to doing things we decide to do is that we're simply "too busy." With so many things on our mind, so many things to do, it's no surprise that we let little details slip by.

But there's a problem with this explanation. After all, how long does it take to write a thank-you note? Five minutes? Ten minutes? Are any of us that busy that we can't take five or ten minutes out of our day to do something as simple as writing a thank-you note?

No! Time itself is usually not the culprit in these situations. For you know as well as I do that when something is truly important, we manage somehow to find the time. And you know as well as I do that there are days when you have hours at your disposal and still never get around to attending to details you really should be attending to.

So the basic question is why don't we *set aside the time* to accomplish these simple tasks?

Now as a psychiatrist, I might be expected to suggest several subconscious reasons for not, say, writing a thank-you note to a couple who has entertained you at their home. Perhaps if we delved deeply enough, we could establish that the host bears a slight resemblance to one of your parents, for whom you harbor a great deal of repressed hostility.

But why complicate matters unnecessarily? The reason you don't get around to writing that thank-you note, and the reason you don't get around to doing all the little tasks I've been alluding to, can be explained very simply: *They never become genuine targets.*

Yes, you get an idea in your head to do these things. In other words, you formulate an intention. But an intention is not a target.

An intention is something you make up your mind to do. A target, however, is something that actually *draws* your attention toward it—that, in a sense, forces a certain line of action.

All targets begin as intentions. But not all intentions become targets. An intention only becomes a target when it assumes certain properties. And usually it's up to you to give these intentions the needed properties.

In this chapter, we'll see how it's done.

The Basics of Target Construction

The first thing you have to do if you want to improve your own targeting skills is to begin to think of all the intentions you formulate as being, in fact, targets. You could think of "intentions" as "goals" instead of "targets," but "target" is a much stronger, much more concrete, much more dynamic concept.

But the fact that we're grouping goals, objectives, intentions, etc., into one category doesn't mean that all targets are equally compelling. They're not. There are important targets and unimportant targets. There are long-range targets and short-range targets. There are targets we pursue for our own pleasure and targets we pursue for the well-being of others.

Once we recognize that not all targets are equally important, we're ready to meet head-on the problem of why we frequently ignore some targets.

The key word here is "priority." For any number of reasons (and, for now, I'm not interested in these reasons), certain targets assume more priority than others, and these are the targets to which we usually address ourselves.

Let's say you wake up one morning with a terrible toothache. Now if it's bad enough, a toothache will virtually demand priority. It will take precedence over most of the other things you may have planned for the day. In the larger scheme of things, it may not mean much to you, but on this day it is a target that literally pounds its way into your consciousness.

But not all targets, of course, have this innate urgency. And that's where you begin to run into problems. For if you want to increase your chances of attending to targets that do not have innate priority, you have to take steps that can increase what might be called the "attention factor" of those targets—steps that will make those less urgent targets stand out more clearly in your mind, cry out more loudly for your attention.

The steps I'm talking about here—and I'll get to them in a minute—don't take the form of promises or resolutions. To formulate an intention, no matter how strongly, isn't the same thing as constructing a target.

Here is where many of us go wrong. We express desires, we formulate intentions. We make resolutions. What we frequently *don't* do, though, is to imbue the object of these desires, intentions, and resolutions with the elements that enhance the chances of our following through on them.

Let me illustrate. Let's assume that the house you live in has a cellar that is at this moment so cluttered that it's nearly impossible to take a step without risking your life. One day, when you waste an hour searching for a screwdriver, you come to the conclusion that the cellar needs cleaning out. And so you make up your mind to do it.

At this stage of the game, what you have is a goal, an objective: a cleaner, well-organized cellar. What you don't have is a genuine target.

What's the difference?

The difference is that the expressed intention to clean up the cellar is just that—an expressed intention, a desire. It has no concreteness, no tangibility. It isn't anything you can set your sights on, or aim at. In short, it's not a target.

Converting this expressed intention into a target isn't as complicated as you may think. It's a matter, first, of identifying those characteristics that typify what we normally associate with targets and giving some of those characteristics to the intentions we express. It's all a matter of target construction.

How to Construct a Target

"Target construction" is the conversion of objectives and goals into genuine targets—into mental forms having the characteristics of targets. For an idea of what these characteristics are, think for a moment about a typical archery target. Such a target has these main characteristics:

1. **It has a definite and permanent place.** An archery target doesn't move around. You know where it is in relation to the shooting line.

2. **It is highly visible.** It stands out very well from the background. You don't have to pick your way through a lot of other visual images to get a fix on it.

3. **It has a bull's-eye.** It gives you something specific to aim at.

The mental targets you construct for yourself must have these same characteristics.

They need a space of their own in your mind.

They have to be visible.

They need a bull's-eye.

So, here we have the three basic steps of target construction—the three steps you take to convert an intention into a target:

1. **Establish a place for the target.**
2. **Create a mental image that is highly visible.**
3. **Paint in a bull's-eye.**

CREATING A TARGET SPACE

As any accomplished cook or carpenter can tell you, it's very difficult to get something done if you don't have adequate space to do it in. Even Cordon Bleu trained chefs would have trouble making a soufflé in a kitchen with insufficient counter space. By the same token, even a master carpenter would have trouble making a precise cut on a work table cluttered with tools and scraps of wood.

In many ways our brain is a work space, too, like the carpenter's shop table or the cook's counter space. The job of the brain is to make decisions, to make choices, to direct our behavior. If the brain is to do this well, it needs to be reasonably free of clutter. If you want your brain to attend to a particular objective, you need space in which to construct the mental image that is to become your target. If there is no available space, you will have to make space.

This brings us to the first step in the conversion process that must take place to create a target out of an objective. I call it *creating a target space.*

Let's go back for a moment to the party situation we talked about in the beginning of the chapter. Driving home in your car, feeling happy about the party you've just attended, the idea of sending a note or gift to your hosts occurs to you. At this stage, you have formulated an intention—the intention to show your appreciation for a pleasant evening. But as long as it stays an intention, the chances of your acting on it are not especially great, and they get slimmer as the days pass. So let's work with the first step in the target construction process—the creation of a space.

It's not a complicated step at all. You can do it while you're waiting for a light to change, or as soon as you get home.

Close your eyes for about 15 seconds and imagine a space being cleared in your mind. Try to visualize an actual scene. Imagine a familiar scene of clutter: a cabinet shelf, a room, a work table. Now visualize yourself making room in the cabinet, the room, or the shelf, moving away the clutter. Clearing a space. Think of your brain as a kind of mental work area. Give yourself room to work in.

Now that you've established a place in your mind for the

target—that is, created a target space—you're ready to go on to the next step: *the creation of a highly visible target.*

SETTING UP A VISIBLE TARGET

Setting up a highly visible target in the space you've just created involves a mental process similar to the process you just used when you created the space. Your aim here is to visualize the target in such a way that it stands up there and says, in effect, "Hit me."

Let's consider the thank-you note you'd like to write. You need a mental picture—a complete mental picture. You need an image of a note pad or a thank-you card. You need a pen. You need a place where you can sit down and compose the note.

Each of these elements is part of the target you are constructing. Each of them must be visualized. Go through the steps in your mind.

See yourself going to the bureau where you keep the thank-you cards. See yourself taking a pen and sitting down at a table. See yourself writing it. See yourself finishing the note, putting it in an envelope, putting a stamp on it, and mailing it. And if you want some bonus reinforcement, *envision your host or hostess actually receiving the note.*

Perhaps you may be thinking that this is a rather complicated piece of business for something as simple as writing a thank-you note. After all, wouldn't it be simpler to take ten minutes as soon as you get home and write the note then and there?

It certainly would, except that for any number of reasons a lot of people can't do this. "I just don't *feel* like writing the note tonight," you say. "I'll do it tomorrow." *Mañana.*

There's nothing wrong with doing it tomorrow—provided you do it tomorrow. But you won't do it unless you've created the mental space and constructed a visible target. For some people, as I've said earlier, the process comes automatically. The recommendations in this book are for people who are not so fortunate.

In any case, this mental construction job I'm talking about doesn't have to take very much time. Maybe a half minute at most. The point is not to cheat. Go through all the steps you can think of. And remember, the more specific you can make the image, the stronger the impact it will have and the stronger its pull on your behavior. This is that mysterious point where the target actually begins to draw your behavior. If the target has been strongly established—mental space for it cleared—and if it has been visualized in all its aspects, there's hardly any way you can avoid hitting it!

PAINTING THE BULL'S-EYE

After you've created a target space and visualized your target in your mind, one final element is called for: a bull's-eye. You need something specific to key on.

What is the bull's-eye?

The bull's-eye I'm talking about is the deadline you set for yourself for pursuing the target. It should be as specific as you can make it. Merely saying to yourself "I'm going to write the thank-you note some time tomorrow" isn't specific enough. Even narrowing it down to "morning" or "afternoon" or "evening" isn't enough of a bull's-eye.

"Tomorrow morning, while I'm waiting for the coffee to brew, I'm going to write the note."

"Tomorrow, as soon as halftime starts on the football game, I'm going to write the note."

In both of these instances, you've given yourself a specific deadline—a genuine bull's-eye to shoot at.

There is, of course, no guarantee that you will hit that bull's-eye. Something unexpected could always come up.

Friends might drop over. An emergency could arise. But chances are that nothing of the kind will happen. Assuming the target deadline you set for yourself is a reasonable one, you will meet it. If you have gone through all the preliminary steps of mentally establishing a space, of constructing a visible target in your mind's eye, and of painting in the bull's-eye, you will achieve it. And to further make sure that you'll achieve the target you've established for yourself, there are a few other practical steps you can take. Let's look at these steps now.

Reinforcing the Target

If a mental target is to do its job, it must remain highly visible for a reasonable length of time. Certain practical steps are often necessary to assure this.

The most common practical step is the little reminder note that gets scrawled on the back of an envelope, or is pinned up on a bulletin board in the kitchen.

WRITE THANK-YOU NOTE TO SIMONS.

For some people, a note like this is sufficient. For most of us, however, it's not. It's a useful reminder—but it's not a bull's-eye. To transform the reminder into a bull's-eye requires additional steps related to the bull's-eye.

Is your target to write the note in the morning while the coffee is brewing? Fine, instead of writing yourself a reminder, get out a note pad and pen the night before and place them in a spot on the kitchen counter where you will see them when you measure out the coffee. If your target deadline was halftime during the Sunday football game, get out the pad and pen and put them near the television set.

What I'm suggesting here is that instead of scattering reminders to yourself, do something specifically related to the job target. Take specific steps that will literally compel you to concentrate your attention on a particular task.

By converting an intention or desire into a genuine target, you take the steps that enhance the chances of your actually addressing yourself to that target. To be sure, there is much more to the targeting process than the simple steps I've outlined in this chapter. But it's with these steps that the process starts. And there are many simple tasks that can be completed with nothing *more* than these few steps.

Don't just take my word for it; see for yourself. Pick out something from your own life—a task, an activity, an intention that, for one reason or another, you haven't found the time to get around to. Go through the three steps of target construction we've been talking about. Create a visual mental space. Convert the objective into a visible target. Give yourself a bull's-eye—a deadline. Then watch and see what happens. I don't think it's unreasonable to promise that within a few days, you'll have launched yourself toward the target you've had so much trouble getting around to. And you will wonder why it took you so long in the first place.

TARGET PRACTICE 2

Determining Targets

How many of the objectives, goals, intentions, and desires in your life at the present time are actually targets? There's an easy way to find out.

Set aside about an hour of your time to prepare a list. On a sheet of paper draw lines for four columns.

In the first column, headed "Targets," list a minimum of five things that you are either trying to accomplish right now or think that you should be trying to accomplish. Then, opposite each item, put a check in one or all of the other three columns headed "Place"; "Visibility"; and "Bull's-Eye."

Where there isn't a check, take the mental steps that will complete the target picture as described in Chapter 2.

CHAPTER 3

Target Sequencing:
A New Look at Planning

 Most of us accept planning as a good idea. We plan our days, our vacations. We get plans drawn up for the work we want done on our houses. We plan specific strategies to deal with specific problems.

But what exactly *is* planning? Or, more to the point, what are the mental steps that go into the process of planning?

If you're like most people, you've probably never given the question much thought. For planning is a process that most of us take for granted, as if the ability to devise a workable plan were something we were born with. A sixth sense. If you're involved with a problem that requires planning, you simply sit down and—well, *plan it.*

But how good at planning are you really?

How well do you understand the mechanics of planning?

How well do you execute these mechanics?

And how skillful are you at devising plans that are not only keyed to what *has* to be done but what you yourself are able to do within the confines of a particular situation?

Finally, how much flexibility do you build into the plans you devise?

In this chapter we're going to examine the planning process within the context of the questions I've just posed. The subject of this chapter is the mechanics of planning, but instead of talking about "planning," we're going to talk about a technique I call *target sequencing.*

What Is Target Sequencing?

To understand target sequencing you need to appreciate, first of all, that targets can usually be divided into two categories: simple and compound.

A *simple target* is any target you can reach in one easy step. You need plane reservations for an upcoming trip. You take a simple step: a call to your travel agent, or to the airlines.

You wake up with a raging toothache. Your simple target is to unburden yourself of the toothache as soon as possible. The one step you take is to make an emergency appointment with your dentist.

A *compound target,* on the other hand, is a target which involves a series of steps. An example of a compound target would be giving a party in your home. Giving a successful party is, in and of itself, a target, but it is made up of a number of smaller targets. Putting together a congenial guest list, sending out the invitations, planning the menu, cleaning the house, ordering the food and beverages, preparing the food, hiring the people to serve and clean up—each of these steps is a target in and of itself; a simple target. But because each of them is related to a larger target, each can be referred to as an *interim target.*

The difference between simple targets and compound targets is not necessarily related to the difficulty of reaching the target. Some "simple" targets are highly challenging. The one step you have to take in order to reach that target can pose great difficulty. Getting a plumber to come to your house to repair a burst pipe is a simple target, but not so simple if it happens to be Christmas Day. Some "compound" targets, on the other hand, are relatively easy to achieve. The reason is that the interim targets are themselves easily accomplished.

The crucial difference between a simple target and a com-

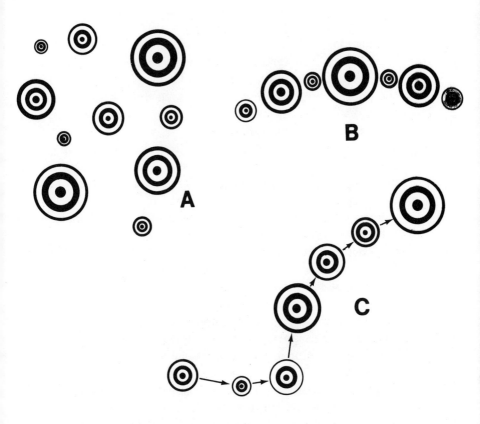

Target sequencing is a way of dealing with an extremely complex situation involving a large number of subsidiary targets. At first (*A*) the targets are all scrambled; it is unclear which are major and which are minor, and there are few clues as to how to order them. Next (*B*) they are laid out in an array so that they can be examined and evaluated; this is, in essence, making a list. Finally (*C*), now properly identified, they are set up in a track—an orderly sequence culminating in the main target being achieved.

pound target is simply that a compound target requires you to arrange interim targets in a certain way. It is this arranging of targets in a certain way that constitutes the process we're looking into in this chapter: target sequencing.

Perhaps you're wondering why we call it "target sequencing" instead of "planning." The main reason is that by using the phrase "target sequencing," we take the process out of the realm of the abstract. "Planning" is a generalized, unspecific term. It is vague and subjective.

Target sequencing is a much more accurate representation of what a plan really should be. For what is a plan, after all, if not a sequence of steps that need to be taken if a particular objective or target has to be reached?

For some people, of course, the substitution of terms makes little or no difference. Whether we call it planning or target sequencing, some people have the ability to identify and to follow a series of logical steps toward the accomplishment of a compound target with ease. Then, too, the more experience you have doing a particular thing, the more likely that you'll be able to go through the completion steps without much trouble. Take the example of giving a party. Some people can put together a sizable party at a week's notice. The guest list is put together, invitations sent out, the food decided on, ordered, and prepared, and it all runs smoothly, like clockwork.

For other people, however, the process is neither smooth nor orderly. It's more like the jumbled movement of a clock with faulty springs. True, the same amount of time and effort—correction, *more* time and effort—may be spent on the same steps, but the overall process is plagued with confusion and tension. The menu is chosen, then changed and rechanged. The guest list keeps changing. A bartender who should have been hired early is not available.

And why? Not because we're "not good" at giving parties. But because we don't follow a logical planning sequence.

We allow our judgment to be clouded by our insecurities and anxieties. In worrying too much about how the food will be, we ignore other aspects of party-giving that are just as important, such as social mix of the guests. In worrying too much about the social mix of the guests, we ignore the food. And, finally, we don't differentiate enough between parties that are being given for close friends or for business associates. We don't recognize the different approaches that work best in each situation.

This is why a clear understanding of the mechanics of planning can be so useful to you. The better you understand these mechanics, the easier it will be for you to overcome the obstacles that often prevent us from sequencing our targets in the most efficient manner possible.

Aiming for the Optimum

It is one thing to draw up a list. It is another thing to devise a plan. Real planning goes beyond the making of a list. It involves the arrangement of steps into a logical order. It involves the logical sequencing of simple targets.

Not that drawing up a list isn't part of the planning process. It is. But the list has to do more than simply enumerate what has to be done. It has to suggest an order in which the steps have to be taken. And here, really, is the difference between a list and a plan. A list tells you what has to be done. A plan tells you not only what has to be done, but the order in which it has to be done.

This brings us to a concept I like to call the *optimum sequence arrangement.*

I wish I could come up with a less formidable phrase, for the idea here is simple. The optimum sequence arrangement is the sequence of simple targets that represents the most efficient and most practical way of achieving the compound target. Most "efficient" and "practical," that is, in the broadest sense of these terms, taking into consideration such factors as time and stress and confusion, as well as reaching the target.

The "optimum" is not a fixed value. Nor is it an arrangement that, once established, never lends itself to modification. It's simply a mental focal point—a concept that helps to anchor the planning process.

The chief advantage of devising a plan with an optimum sequence arrangement is that it reduces the chances of duplicated effort. If you lived in Washington, D.C., for instance, and had to make a business trip to Baltimore, Philadelphia, and New York, you wouldn't travel first to Philadelphia, then south to Baltimore, and then north again to New York. You'd try to arrange your schedule so that you wouldn't have to retrace your steps. The same principle holds true for any plan you might make. Ideally, you want a sequence arrangement that doesn't oblige you to retrace your steps, to duplicate your effort, to waste your time and energy.

Of course, it's not always possible to follow an optimum target sequence in your planning. In an illogical world, strict rules of logic cannot always be applied. Let's say, for instance, that your business required that you have appointments in Philadelphia the first day, Baltimore the second, and New York the third. This sequence of targets may not be the most practical or efficient, but for reasons of the business at hand, it will be necessary.

So remember, arranging targets according to their optimum sequence is a guideline, not a rigid law to be followed no matter what the circumstances. Nevertheless, whenever you sit down to draw up a plan, you should be aware of the ideal: an *optimum sequence arrangement,* and you should build your plan as much as you can around such an arrangement.

The Mechanics of Target Sequencing

The mechanics of target sequencing can be broken down into two steps:

1. **Break down the compound target into a series of interim targets.**
2. **Arrange those targets in the optimum sequence.**

SPREADING OUT THE PIECES

An experienced jigsaw puzzle fan knows that the first thing you do when you are working on a puzzle is to spread out all the pieces of the puzzle in front of you, right side up. The idea is to be able to *see* all the pieces you have to work with.

The same principle applies to target sequencing. Before you can start to think about *arranging* targets in a logical or optimum sequence, you first of all need a reasonably clear idea of what interim targets you have to work with.

The biggest mistake people make in planning is to start the construction process before all the parts they must work with are recognized and understood.

Here's an example: You've just been nominated as chairperson of a food committee for an upcoming function at your social club, church group—whatever. You happen to know a couple of caterers quite well, so you call them. When you get the caterer on the phone you suddenly realize you don't have all the information you need. You forgot to take the time to find out what cooking facilities will be available, where the dinner is being held. You're embarrassed to discover you don't even know how many people may attend.

There's nothing catastrophic about making calls this way, but the point is that you're going to have to make those calls again. So all you've done, unless you have a specific reason for making the calls, is to make extra work for yourself.

One of the reasons this kind of thing happens is that whenever we are faced with a compound target, we become anxious to "get cracking." We want to start seeing results early. We don't like things hanging over our heads.

It's good to get a fast start on compound targets, but the

problems that pop up when you start taking actions prematurely, before you've gathered all possible information, can—and often do—haunt you later on.

Not long ago I got a lesson in this when I had some carpentry work done in my office. For the first two days, not a nail was hammered. Had the carpenter not come to me highly recommended, I might have figured him to be a very slow worker. He wasn't slow at all. He wasn't wasting time as he measured, figured, considered alternate ways to do the remodeling. He was *saving* time, spreading out the pieces of his particular puzzle. He was a careful and experienced carpenter who had learned that by taking extra time in the beginning to plan out each job, he would not have to waste a lot of time going back and forth to the lumberyard at the last minute.

Let's apply the same principle to you. You have a task to perform—a compound target to reach. What do you do?

First of all, sit down and give it some careful thought. Get a piece of paper and make a list of all the interim targets that have to be reached in order to reach the compound target. Careful! Don't start on any of these targets until your list is as complete as you can make it. A nervous voice inside you may prod you to get started, to take some action, but don't let it propel you into action prematurely. First, get all the pieces of the puzzle spread out in front of you, everything you can think of.

Once you've analyzed and established all the interim targets that need to be reached if you are ready to attain the compound target, you're ready to take the next step: *sequencing*.

In some targeting situations, the sequence of the interim targets will be of no consequence. It won't matter which of the interim targets you reach first or which of the interim targets you reach last. If you have five rooms in your house that need cleaning, it probably doesn't matter all that much which room you start to clean first. You'll reach your final target—getting the house ready—in the same amount of time and you'll expend the same amount of energy.

In many cases, too, the sequence will be so obvious that you'll hardly have to think about it. This is often the case when you're cooking, when you can't proceed with one step in the recipe unless you've already completed another.

But in many targeting situations, sequencing has a paramount bearing on the amount of time and effort that must go into the reaching of a target. There are many situations in which the targeting is *not* self evident. These situations frequently crop up in your job. They often crop up when you have a problem at home. These are the situations in which you have to make various judgments in order to arrive at an optimum sequence. And when the time comes to make these judgments, two principles, above all, should guide efforts. One of them is *priority*. The other is something that can best be described as *economy of effort*. Let's look now at how both of these considerations fit into the target sequencing process.

PRIORITY, ECONOMY OF EFFORT, AND SEQUENCING

If there is one key to successful target sequencing, it is the ability to combine the concepts of priority and economy of effort. By priority, we're talking about the relative importance of interim targets. By economy of effort, we're talking about the amount of time and effort required to reach an interim target in relation to its place in the target sequence.

As a general rule you will always want to place the high-priority interim targets toward the front of your sequence, but with this condition: that the placing of the target in this sequence doesn't overly affect the economy of your effort.

For example, most men are probably more comfortable facing the world without a shirt on than without their trousers.

This is another way of saying that in the sequence of interim targets that make up the larger target of getting dressed, trousers have more priority than a shirt. On the other hand, if a man puts his trousers on first, he's only going to have to undo the belt and the zipper once more when he puts on his shirt. Obviously, if he puts his shirt on first, then the trousers, he will only have to do up the belt and zipper once.

We're dealing here with *general* principles, not laws chiseled in stone. Priority and economy of effort are abstract concepts. Their relative importance will vary from situation to situation and from person to person. What is easy for you to do may not be easy for me to do. What may have high priority for me may not have high priority for you.

Another thing. There are some targeting situations in which it doesn't pay to worry about sequencing at all—situations in which the best thing to do is simply to roll up your sleeves and deal with each individual problem as it comes along.

But generally, most of the situations you encounter that require planning will lend themselves to the target sequencing concepts we've just talked about. The sequencing process is mainly a matter of learning how to balance the two variables: *priority* and *economy of effort.*

Remember the general principle: Interim targets of priority should come early in the sequence except in those cases where their place has an effect on economy of effort.

THE SEQUENCING PROCESS: AN ILLUSTRATION

The best way to illustrate how the principles of *target sequencing* work is to set up an actual situation. Let us assume that good fortune has smiled upon you and has presented you with the possibility of a one-month stay at a private home in the south of France. There's only one hitch: You have less than two weeks to prepare for it.

Now the worst thing you can do in a situation like this—

and it's something most people do—is to run out and start doing things in random fashion. Unless you happen to be one of those fortunate persons with an instinctive sense of sequencing, the chances are that the next two weeks will be pure torture for you.

Let's not panic. You have a tool. This book. You are not making hurried, last-minute plans for a trip. You are *sequencing interim targets*. And your first step should be the step a careful carpenter always takes when he starts out on a job: making a careful assessment of all the elements necessary in completing the job. Or, as we've said, spreading out all the pieces of the puzzle.

Set aside an hour or so for this analysis. Get a piece of paper and a pen. Spread out all the pieces. What you're doing, of course, is setting up your *interim targets*.

I can think of any number of interim targets right off the top of my head. I'll list them here without any order of importance. We can get to that later.

- Air tickets to France
- Kennel arrangements for the dog and cat
- Passports
- Notification of post office to stop mail delivery
- Notification of newspaper service to suspend delivery
- Cancellation of dental and doctor (or any other) appointments that fall during the time of your absence
- Someone to water your plants and check the house while you're gone
- Transportation to and from the airport
- New bathing suits for the children, and for you and your spouse
- A French phrase book
- A list of good restaurants from friends who know the area you'll be visiting
- A new piece of luggage
- Packing for the trip

Here are thirteen interim targets, all of which come under the larger target of "preparing for the trip." Now let's "sequence" these targets in a way that will meet the conditions we've already established: *priority* and *economy of effort.*

Let's start with priority.

Not all of the fourteen interim targets listed are *absolutely essential* to the trip. So let's separate the more important targets from the less important targets.

Several time and efficiency experts over the past few years have developed systems for setting up plans of action on the basis of priorities. Many of these systems use numbers (1 to 10, 1 to 5, etc.) to rank important priorities, reasonably important priorities, and not-so-important priorities.

Because I like to keep things as simple as possible, I recommend a simple system using circles. An interim target of the highest priority gets three circles. The next important group receives two circles. The last and least important group would receive one circle.

Now it's obvious that a certain amount of subjectivity necessarily will creep into the selection process, so don't strive for complete objectivity. Rely on common sense.

Here's what a one-circle, two-circle, and three-circle grouping might look like:

000 Priorities:
Air tickets to France
Passports
Transportation to and from airport
Packing
Kennel arrangements for the dog and cat

00 Priorities:
Post office notification
Newspaper delivery suspension
Arranging for someone to check house and water the plants
Cancellation of doctor, dental, and business appointments
A new piece of luggage

0 Priorities:
Restaurant list
Phrase book
Bathing suits

Let's talk for a moment about the assignment of these priorities. You'll notice that all of the three-circle targets are targets without which the trip could not take place. Tickets, passports, kennel arrangements, etc.—without them, you couldn't go. The two-circle targets are important but not absolutely essential. The cancellation of the doctor and dental appointments, for instance, could be done by letter once you're in France. Ideally, you will get to these priorities before you leave. All we're trying to do here, remember, is establish an orderly sequence. As for the one-circle targets, none of them will seriously affect the trip if not achieved.

It may seem to many of you that I am belaboring the obvious. Yet I know people who, if presented with the situation just described, would rush out the first day and waste an afternoon looking for a bathing suit or chasing after the best phrase book. These two things could, of course, have a higher priority than I've given them. The crucial thing, however, is to be absolutely certain that the essential priorities are not ignored until the last moment.

There's a simple question you can ask yourself to determine whether an interim target belongs in the three-circle category:

Could the trip take place if this target is not reached?

If the answer is "no," you have a three-circle interim target.

If the answer is "yes," another question should help you to determine whether it belongs in the two- or one-circle classification.

If I don't reach this target, will it cause me problems?

If the answer here is "yes," you have a two-circle interim target.

WORKING WITHIN THE PRIORITY GROUPS

Once you've divided your interim targets into priority categories, the sequencing procedure is well on its way. But there's still a way to go. First of all, we can establish priorities within each priority group. The main criterion for choice here is timing. Look back at the list. There are five interim targets in the three-circle grouping. With a moment's thought you can see that timing is not equally crucial in each. It takes about a week at least to get a passport but only an hour or two, usually, to arrange for a kennel. For this reason, it is wise to put getting your passport ahead of vaccinations in the sequence. Then, too, it's obvious that packing, as important as it is, cannot be done until the last few days, and so it naturally falls toward the end of the sequence.

There's one more factor that must be taken into consideration. I call it the "deadline" factor. Under normal circumstances, the rule here is simple: *the longer the estimated time it will take to reach an interim target, the higher up in the sequence hierarchy you should place it—but with one exception.* When a particular target *has* to be reached at a particular time, that is, there is a deadline involved, then that target must take precedence. It's possible, for instance, that heavy bookings on the airlines would make it imperative that you see about your airline ticket before doing anything else.

Again, we're talking here about *general* principles. The last thing I want to do is create the impression that the reaching of compound targets obliges you to lock yourself into a rigid sequence of interim targets that should never be tampered with. You have to remain flexible. You have to exercise judgment. Furthermore, you always have to be prepared to deal with the unexpected.

That said, we can now turn to the second principle of target sequencing—economy of effort.

PIGGYBACK TARGETING: DOING MORE IN LESS TIME

Do you know the old joke about the three men who come into a grocery store together? It's simple-minded, perhaps, but it's a good illustration of what I'm talking about. One of them asks for a pound of nuts, obliging the clerk to get a ladder, climb to a top shelf, get the can, come down the ladder, measure out the nuts, climb back up the ladder, put the can back, come down the ladder. After he's done all this he turns to the next man. The second man also asks for a pound of nuts. This time the clerk is clever. Instead of climbing up to get the nuts, he asks the third man, "And what about you? Do you want a pound of nuts, too?"

"No," the man says.

So the clerk climbs up, gets the nuts, climbs down, measures them, and returns them. When he's finished he turns to the third man, who says, "I'd just like a *half* a pound of nuts!"

You can see what I'm driving at. The situation in the joke is unlikely to happen to any of us. Yet it would be almost impossible to calculate the number of hours the average person wastes on unnecessary and extraneous effort. Intelligent sequencing can eliminate a good deal of extraneous effort, but you have to be alert to the possibilities. You can almost make a game of it.

Let's go back to our three-circle list (Get passport, airline tickets, etc.). A sequence has been established on the basis of timing. Now it's time to ask yourself another question:

How many of these targets can I hit at the same time?

How many targets, in other words, can be piggybacked?

A couple of possibilities come to mind immediately. Can you get your passport and a vaccination on the same day? Possibly. And, while you're phoning for the plane reserva-

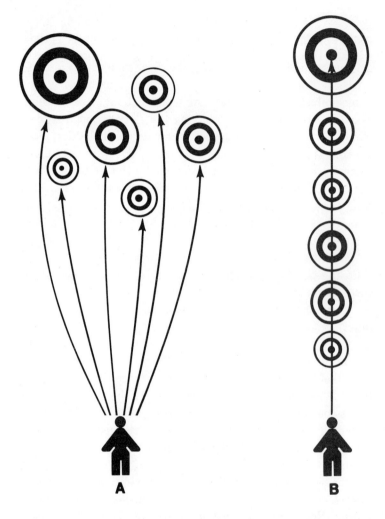

Piggyback targeting is one technique for dealing with a situation in which there is a complex set of targets that require considerable energy to reach (*A*). They must be organized so that they can be reached by a few relatively simple activities (*B*). This is killing many birds with one stone.

tions, why not handle your airport transportation as well—
and, for that matter, the kennel arrangements, too.

There is always a danger, admittedly, that in trying to piggyback too many targets at once, you'll overburden yourself.
But if there is an art to sequencing, it lies in the ability to recognize and take advantage of target piggybacking possibilities. In many instances, the possibilities will be obvious—
once you look for them. You will see that while you're involved with one target, you can go after a second target with
very little effort. It may very well be that you can reach into
the two- and one-circle category before you've finished all of
your three-circle targets. If there is a bookshop next door to
the passport office, there's no reason you can't take a few
minutes extra and pick up the phrase book. Use your good
judgment. But always keep in mind that piggyback targeting
is only a viable concept when the added effort to reach the
"added" target is minimal.

SUMMING UP

What I have tried to do in this chapter is to present a new
way of looking at an old subject: planning. There is no mys-
tery to good planning, even though people who are good at it
are generally unaware of the actual steps they take to produce good, workable plans. Viewing planning as a targeting
process can help to put the process in a more functional
framework. Then, if you think of a plan as a series of interim
targets that differ from one another in importance and
should be sequenced according to their priority and relation
to economy of effort, you may be able to change the image
you have of yourself as a person who "can't plan well." And,
as I have been saying all along, a plan is not a behavioral
strait jacket. It is a behavioral tool that, like any tool, is of no
use unless you utilize it properly.

TARGET PRACTICE 3

Improving Target-Sequencing Skills

The following target exercise is meant primarily for those of you who've never actually sat down and planned an entire project. The purpose of the exercise is to improve your target sequencing skills.

The compound target we're going to be concerned with in this exercise is getting the basement into shape. Here's what to do.

1. Get a sheet of paper and a pen or pencil.
2. On the paper, write a list of all the various chores that have to be done if the cellar is to be cleaned, such as clearing debris, cleaning the floor, etc. Leave a space or several lines between each listed item.
3. Under the various subtargets (i.e., chores) list what has to be done before each particular subtarget can be pursued. An obvious example would be that the floor has to be cleared before you can start to clean it, and that it has to be swept before it can be mopped.
4. Based on this new sublisting, set a sequence, keeping in mind that your principal aim here is to reduce duplication of activity.
5. Piggyback chores wherever possible.

Remember, this is merely an exercise. Its purpose is to give you an idea of how sitting down and sequencing a project can help you to simplify your approach to compound targets.

CHAPTER 4

Scheduling Can Make a Difference

Of all the unnoticed elephants that thunder around in our behavioral repertoire, none is as potentially valuable, or as under-utilized, as the power we all possess to schedule—to organize our time in a way that is best tailored to our particular needs and wants. It isn't possible to control the number of targets you have to pursue at any given time, but as busy as you may be, you probably have more flexibility than you realize in determining exactly how to organize your time in the pursuit of those targets.

Don't underestimate this power. More often than you might imagine, it isn't necessarily *what* you do or *how* you do it that determines whether or not you reach a target. Sometimes it's a simple question of *when* you do it, of how you organize your time. The sales report that took you five hours to prepare on a Tuesday afternoon might have taken only an hour if you'd done it the following morning, when you were not as tired, didn't have as many distractions, or had access to information you didn't have the previous afternoon. Similarly, the faucet repair job that took you half of Tuesday evening might have taken you only half an hour if you had tackled it over the weekend, when you weren't as preoccupied with other concerns, and when you had the right wrench to work with.

Any number of variables, independent of what has to be done and how well equipped you are to do it, can influence your performance in any given situation. Your moods, your energy level, your work load—all these fluctuating elements very much affect your ability to hit your targets. True, you don't always have the liberty to tailor your schedule *around* these variables, but the possibility for such tailoring is present more often than you may think. It's simply a matter of getting the most out of these possibilities, of being in control *of* your time, not being controlled *by* it. No behavioral tool you possess is more useful.

Taking a New Look at Scheduling

Before going any further, let's clear up some of the myths and misconceptions that some people have about scheduling. To begin with, scheduling doesn't mean that you must place yourself at the mercy of a time clock. It doesn't mean constantly checking your watch, nervously concerned every moment as to whether you are "on" schedule. Nor does it mean that you are putting yourself inside a behavioral straight jacket, or forcing yourself to do things you don't want to do simply for the sake of following a schedule.

No, scheduling doesn't automatically eliminate spontaneity from your life. To the contrary, a schedule—if it's well designed—can be a liberating influence in your life. Organizing your time more efficiently gives you more time than you now have to enjoy yourself, more time to be spontaneous. Indeed, a schedule that doesn't allow for some spontaneity is not a successful schedule.

Another thing about scheduling I want to emphasize is that scheduling isn't a tool you use in one area of your life and discard in other areas. "I'm a very organized person," a lawyer who came to see me told me not long ago. To prove his point, he presented me with an appointment book filled solidly from early morning to early evening with scheduled appointments and meetings. But when I asked him what about time set aside for family, for recreation, for work around the house, the lawyer told me, "I don't need to schedule *those* things. I take care of them when I have the time."

Which, of course, was part of the lawyer's problem. He didn't have the time for these other areas of his life because he didn't think it was necessary to *make* the time. Like many people, he took for granted that he didn't have to work into his daily schedule those aspects of his life that weren't tied to his job. So he never had any time to unwind or relax. And it was affecting his relationship with his children.

This is why I want to stress throughout this chapter the importance of scheduling, not only as it relates to any particular area of your life—your job, for instance—but also as it relates to your total life. But don't worry. Putting more overall organization into your life is not as difficult as you may think. And the rewards far outnumber the drawbacks. To be more effective in your life, to be more successful in reaching your targets, to derive more joy from the life process—you don't have to make wholesale changes in your life to realize these aims. The trick may well lie in nothing more complicated than a simple reorganization of how you work—and play—each day.

Evaluating Your Present Schedule

Even if you've never sat down and actually planned out a day or a week, chances are you're already on a schedule of one kind or another. You probably wake up at the same time every day, and go to work at the same time. Chances are you eat your meals at roughly the same time, and go to bed at pretty much the same hour every night.

It's quite possible that the schedule or routine you have settled into over the years works well for you. Many people, either by "instinct" or by trial and error, have developed a schedule that well suits their particular life-style and their particular personality.

Then again, it may be that your present schedule isn't working as much in your behalf as it could or should. Think about it a moment.

Are you as productive as you'd like to be on a day-in and day-out basis—as productive as you think you *should* be?

Are you as tension-free as you'd like to be? Do you have the time you need to relax, to spend time with people you care about, to do the things you want to do?

The answers you give to each of these questions may well be determined by the kind of schedule you're presently following.

I am using "schedule" in the broadest sense of the term. When and what you eat, when and how long you sleep, the relative amounts of time you spend working, playing, interacting with other people, reading, thinking—all these activities make a difference in what you derive from life. The amount of time devoted to any or all of them is important in determining the quality of your life. And because nearly everything you do in the course of a day determines the quality of your life on that particular day, everything you do should play a part in the decisions you make concerning the organization of that day.

This brings us to what I consider the most important element in scheduling: balance. The aim of a good schedule is to allow you to meet not just one or two of your needs, but to let you satisfy or come close to satisfying all of your individual needs. Since your time is limited, a proper schedule must be one which balances your needs in the optimum way. It isn't always practical to set up a schedule that satisfies all your diverse needs on a *daily* basis, but I don't think it's asking too much of a schedule to meet your needs on a *weekly* basis.

Does *your* schedule do this? Are you currently following a general routine that provides your life with the balance necessary for you to derive everything you want from your life? Are some things which "you always mean to get around to" nearly always neglected? To help give you an idea of just how balanced your schedule really is, here is a quick test you can take. The idea behind these questions is to measure the overall balance in your present schedule. For each of the questions, select the one answer that most closely describes your present situation: pick just one for each question.

1. During a typical week in your life, do you generally accomplish:
   a. Everything you set out to accomplish?
   b. Most of what you set out to accomplish?
   c. About half of what you set out to accomplish?
   d. Much less than you set out to accomplish?
   e. The question doesn't apply to me because I don't set targets for myself.

If you answered a, give yourself 4 points; b, 2 points; c, 1 point; d, no points, and e, minus 2 points. In subsequent questions, the point total (plus or minus) will follow the answer.

2. Throughout a typical week in your life, particularly during the workday, are you usually:
   a. Relaxed and on top of things? (+1)
   b. Sometimes relaxed, sometimes edgy? (+1)
   c. Often harried and under pressure but able to handle it? (−1)
   d. Nearly always tense and harried and usually upset because of it? (−3)

3. Do you ever get the feeling that the more you try to do, the less you get done?
   a. Hardly. (+4)
   b. Occasionally. (+2)
   c. Frequently. (−1)
   d. Almost always. (−3)

4. When it comes to keeping appointments are you:
   a. Almost always on time? (+3)
   b. Occasionally late but never for important things? (+1)
   c. Usually a little bit late for most appointments? (0)
   d. Almost always late and sometimes as much as a half hour? (−3)

5. When something important but unexpected comes up, how easy is it for you to work it into your schedule?
   a. Fairly easy to work it into both daily and weekly schedule. (+3)
   b. Easy to work it into weekly schedule, given a few days notice, but difficult to work into daily schedule. (0)
   c. Difficult to work into either daily or weekly schedule. (−1)
   d. Nearly impossible to work it into either daily or weekly schedule. (−4)

6. During a typical week, do you skip or rush through meals (especially lunch)?
   a. Rarely. (+2)
   b. Occasionally. (+1)
   c. Frequently. (−1)
   d. Almost always. (−3)

7. Do unexpected distractions frequently make it difficult for you to concentrate on one thing at a time?
   a. Rarely. (+3)
   b. Occasionally. (+1)
   c. Frequently. (−1)
   d. Almost always. (−3)

8. Do small, unattended details—phone calls, letters, etc.—have a tendency to pile up?
   a. Rarely. (+4)
   b. On occasion. (+2)
   c. Sometimes. (+1)
   d. Much of the time. (−2)
   e. Very often. (−4)

9. When you finish working on a typical day, do you have difficulty relaxing?
   a. Rarely. (+3)
   b. Sometimes. (+1)
   c. Frequently. (−2)
   d. Nearly always. (−4)

10. How often during a typical week do you find yourself having to repeat tasks you've already addressed yourself to at least once?
    a. Rarely. (+3)

b. Sometimes. (+1)
c. Frequently. (−2)
d. Almost always. (−4)

HOW TO RATE YOURSELF

A "perfect" score in the test you've just taken would be 32. This would indicate that you are not only an extremely well-organized person, but that you are well in control of your life. Frankly, there's little I can tell you that can improve this facet of your behavior, but chances are you scored less than 20. Here, in general, is how you can rate yourself.

20 or over. If you scored 20 or better in this test, you're probably operating on a highly productive, well-organized schedule. If you have no complaints about the way your life is going, there's no need to make any major changes in the organization of your time.

14 to 19. A score between 14 and 19 indicates a better-than-average level of organization, but with room for improvement. Chances are the changes you'll have to make to realize this improvement are minimal.

8 to 13. If your score is between 8 and 13, you can consider yourself average. You have a lot of room for improvement. To realize this improvement you'll probably have to do some reorganization of your present schedule.

2 to 7. A 2 to 7 score is a fairly accurate sign that your present schedule is in need of some major overhauling.

1 or below zero. If your score in this was 1 or below zero, it's a wonder you found the time to read this book. A score in this area indicates that there is virtually no organization in your life. If, despite this total lack of organization, you consider yourself productive and fulfilled, it means one of two things: 1. You're a genius; 2. You probably didn't answer the questions properly.

Scheduling the Basic Ingredients

Two principles, above all, underlie the creation of an effective schedule. One is an understanding of the targets that are operational in your life at any given time. The other principle is an understanding of yourself.

TARGET ANALYSIS

One of the biggest pitfalls many people fall into in trying to organize their time is not being aware of all the demands that a particular task may call for at a particular time. The average person generally thinks in terms of how long it will take to attend to a particular target: how long a meeting will take, how long it will take to prepare a meal or finish a report. But what people too often ignore is the amount of effort and concentration it will take to reach that particular target, and the degree of stress the target embodies.

I'm thinking now of Helen P., a divorced career woman. For a while Helen was setting aside a half hour or so two nights a week to help her nine-year-old daughter with math homework. There's nothing unusual about a parent setting aside a half hour a couple of days a week to help a child out with schoolwork, but Helen underestimated the amount of mental effort and stress that this particular half hour with her child would entail. Helen was an exacting, impatient woman who probably should not have been working with her child, anyway, and certainly not after a full day at her job, which was with a publishing house. Yet Helen was constantly berating herself for not being able to "stay patient." "There must be something wrong with me," she once said. "Why can't I keep my patience for just 30 minutes?"

Helen's problem is a common one. It stems from not being able to differentiate clearly enough two different types of targets: 1. *effort-intensive targets,* and 2. *time-intensive targets.* Helping her daughter with math homework was not a "time-intensive" target—it only involved thirty minutes— but it *was* an "effort-intensive" target. That is, it required a sustained amount of patience and concentration—more, it turned out, than Helen was able to summon on weekday evenings.

RECOGNIZING EFFORT-INTENSIVE TARGETS

Time-intensive targets are simple to recognize and therefore simple to work into a schedule. If you know a meeting is going to take five hours, you can block out a five-hour time segment. No problem.

But effort-intensive targets are trickier to deal with. Indeed, it is the inability to schedule adequately effort-intensive targets that lies at the root of much of the stress that many busy people have to deal with on a day-to-day basis.

Bear in mind it isn't the time involved or even the nature of a target that makes it effort intensive. It's more a matter of what reaching that target takes out of you, physically or mentally. And it's highly subjective.

Traveling is a good example. For most people, a plane trip is a routine experience—so routine that some executives manage to get a lot of work done on an airplane. But I know a lawyer who has always been uneasy about flying and almost invariably arrives at his destination anxious and exhausted. So for him, going somewhere on a plane is an effort-intensive experience. It takes a lot out of him.

What is the advantage of differentiating targets on this basis?

The chief advantage is that it helps you to achieve a sense of psychological balance in your schedule. If you don't take into consideration the effort intensiveness of a target, there's a good possibility that some segments of your schedule may get overloaded with effort-intensive targets. But by recognizing the effort-intensive factor, you can balance your schedule out—that is, keep effort-intensive targets separate from each other so that you're attending to these targets when you are best prepared to deal with them.

Consider the change Helen P., the divorced career woman, made in her schedule to better avoid the conflicts she was having with her daughter over math homework. Nothing complicated. Helen simply rescheduled the math sessions for Sunday evening. Why Sunday evening? Because Sunday was a day on which Helen had no other effort-intensive targets to deal with.

Or consider how recognizing the same principle made a difference to the airplane-shy lawyer I spoke of earlier. By changing his schedule around so that he arrived the night before a business meeting instead of the morning of a business meeting, the lawyer was able to approach his business meetings in a much calmer and clearer state of mind.

In neither of the above examples was a particular target abandoned. The only thing that changed was the place of that target in the person's overall schedule.

We're dealing here, of course, with a highly relative concept. In Helen's case, there were weekday evenings when she was able to work effectively with her child. But almost always, these were the evenings that followed days in which things went smoothly at the office. Helen had no way of predicting from day to day how much stress she would have to deal with at the office, no way of knowing what her frame of mind would be when she sat down to work with her daughter at night. Which is why it was a mistake to schedule this particular target on a weekday night.

Not that this is an uncommon practice among busy people. Over the years, I've had as patients dozens of overstressed executives. If there is one thing that nearly all of them have had in common, it is their habit of overscheduling effort-intensive tasks. It amazes me sometimes that well-educated, highly intelligent men and women don't recognize that the supply of mental energy we carry with us is no more inexhaustible than the supply of physical energy we have at our disposal. Common sense tells us that after you've run for, say, six miles, you're not ready to play two hours of tennis. Your body needs time to recover. The same principle holds true for mental tasks. Just as we all differ in our physical capacities and tolerances, so do we differ in our mental capacities and tolerances, and none of us is a superman or superwoman in either respect. Our bodies need "recovery time" after a vigorous workout. So do our minds. To ignore the need for such a period is to abuse yourself in very much the same way you would abuse yourself if you were to overextend yourself physically.

"Optimal Performance Time"

If you're like most people, there are certain times of the day when it is easier for you to get things done than at other times of the day. I myself happen to be a "morning" person: I am sharper mentally in the morning than I am in the afternoon or evening. On the other hand, I know a writer who is much more productive and creative late at night than at any other time.

There is nothing unusual about these patterns. It's only natural that our energy levels throughout the day fluctuate in ways that relate to our life styles and our metabolism.

What about you? What are your "optimum" times? Morning? Afternoon? When do you generally feel the most energetic? When are you the most productive? If you think about it—or better still, monitor yourself for a few days—you should be able to get some idea of when you do your best work, and once you have established your optimum performance time, a time when you think more clearly and perform more energetically, it would be foolish not to take advantage of this discovery. The general rule is this: When you are scheduling a day—or even an entire week—try to arrange your schedule so that you can attend to effort-intensive targets at those times when you are best able to generate your maximum effort.

One man I know who has mastered this principle of scheduling is Peter K., a successful publishing executive. Indeed, Peter maintains that his understanding of his own "optimum performance" time is the one factor that more than any other makes him more productive than his co-workers. This is his method.

"If I can, the only time of the day when I schedule really important meetings or commit myself to important decisions is between 9:30 and 11:00 each morning. I usually get to the office by 9:00 and it takes me about a half hour to get myself geared up. At 9:30 I'm fresh and eager and I feel a greater sense of energy and confidence than I do at any other time of the day. My 'low' point is usually midafternoon—maybe an hour after I've come back from lunch. That's the time of the day I set aside to handle the less important details of my job that don't require too much in the way of concentration."

You can apply this method to your own situation.

Look at *your* job or *your* daily schedule of activities. Chances are that not all of your activities or tasks require the same degree of mental energy or sharpness. So, if possible, schedule effort-intensive tasks for those times of the day when you are best able to attend to them. Let's say it's a Tuesday and you have targets that have to be reached by the end of the day: 1. You have to complete the seating chart for an upcoming organization luncheon; 2. You have to do the weekly marketing list.

Each of these targets has to be completed by the end of the day. But the completion of the seating chart will require more effort from you than the shopping. So you should slot that activity in what you feel is your "optimal performance time." The principle never changes. *The more difficult or challenging the task, the more you should try to slot that task into a time when you can bring to the task the full measure of your mental capabilities.*

Energy-level differences are only one of many elements that need to be taken into account when you organize a schedule truly tailored to your individual needs. Every aspect in your life must be considered and acknowledged. The kind of job you have, how far you live from your job, your marital situation, the number and the ages of the children you have, the kind of hobbies you have—each of these things differentiates you from the next person. Each has a bearing on the kind of schedule you make for yourself.

One of the main reasons that many of us *don't* take these individual factors into consideration enough is that we allow habit and conditioning to govern our thinking. Not too long ago, I had a conversation with a woman in her mid-thirties who was having a difficult time adjusting to a new job. She was married and had three school-aged children. She had not worked full time outside the home since the early days of her marriage, before she had had children. Like many women in this situation, she was trying her best not to let the job interfere with what she felt were her duties as a homemaker and mother.

As you might expect, she wasn't doing a very good job at it, and for an obvious reason: If you're working full time, it's virtually impossible to devote as much time and energy to your household chores and your family as you would if you weren't working full time. Prior to taking the job, this woman had always prided herself on the meals she prepared for her family, and she was determined to maintain her high standards. This determination was the chief source of her problem.

In her case, the schedule adjustment was simple enough. But first she had to demand less of herself as a homemaker. Eventually, she made a decision to simplify the meals she served and to organize her time accordingly. But the schedule adjustment came only after she recognized that a woman working full time outside the home can't follow effectively the same heavy schedule at home as a woman who has a part time job or none at all.

The example I've just given may seem obvious, but it nonetheless illustrates a concept that many people can utilize more effectively. Let the schedule you organize for yourself reflect *your* needs and *your* situation, not the needs and situation of somebody else. It's clear that whatever schedule you adopt for yourself must take into account the targets present in your job and in your home responsibilities, but frequently you can arrange these targets in a manner best suited to *you*.

Years ago, many housewives set aside certain days of the week for certain tasks. You washed clothes on Monday, ironing was done on Tuesday, and the marketing was done on Wednesday. Some people still operate according to these schedules, even though it is inconvenient. There's no law that tells you when you have to clean your house, or do the laundry, or take care of the marketing; no law that dictates when you have to deal with your correspondence or work on job reports. And there's no law that tells you when you have to eat or go to sleep or wake up. These are all basic areas of your life in which you have much more control than you realize. You can schedule them according to the targets that you want to reach, not according to what other people do.

Don't be afraid to experiment. The woman mentioned above found her life immensely easier once she got her family accustomed to eating dinner at 7 P.M. instead of an hour earlier as they had when she wasn't working. It took a couple of days for her children to get used to the new schedule but after that there was no problem, and the extra hour gave her the time she needed to make the transition from working woman to mother.

Target overload (*A*) occurs when there are so many targets piled up that most are distorted, many even hidden.
The solution (*B*): spread them out in a number of arrays
so that you can respond to them in an orderly way. Most
will regain their proper shapes.

WHERE DO YOU GO FROM HERE?

Understanding the demands of the various targets in your life and understanding your own working characteristics are two of the most important factors in scheduling. But there is more to scheduling than applying these two factors. In the next chapter, we'll look into some other specific elements that can help you organize your time more productively.

TARGET PRACTICE 4

Avoiding "Effort-Intensive" Target Overload

This exercise requires nothing more than paper and pen and a copy of your appointment book (if you have one). Find a "typical" day. Now jot down each of the activities you had scheduled for that day. If the activity was a time-intensive target, mark a "T." If it was an effort-intensive target, mark an "E." (Some targets, of course, are both, in which case you'll mark down both letters.)

If the list you prepared is top-heavy with either "T"s or "E"s, it could mean that you're not sensitive enough to the difference between a time-intensive target and an effort-intensive target. This lack of awareness could be interfering with your ability to work at peak efficiency throughout the day.

CHAPTER 5

How To Be Busy and Productive: Multitrack Scheduling

You've probably heard the adage that if you need something important to get done, find a busy person to do it. The logic here, of course, is that getting things done isn't so much a matter of how much time you have to do things, but how you use this time. And busy people generally tend to be people who know how to use their time productively.

Well, almost.

I have no quarrel with the above adage insofar as it goes. Certainly there are a great many busy people who use their time productively.

But there also are a great many people for whom being "busy" is a target in and of itself—the kind of people who are always on the go, who never have a free moment yet never seem to get anything done. And this isn't to mention the busy people who are indeed productive but not without paying a high price. I'm talking here about the workaholic—the man or woman so wrapped up in his or her work that other aspects of life suffer because of it.

All of which is to emphasize the point that you shouldn't confuse being "busy" and "working hard" with target-oriented behavior. The three don't necessarily go together. You can be busy without being productive. You can be productive without reaching your targets.

The ideal here is to be busy and productive, and productive in a way that doesn't force you to sacrifice your health, your psychological well-being, your relationships with your family and your friends. There are many elements that go into reaching this ideal. One of them lies in a target-related skill I call multitrack targeting.

How Multitrack Targeting Works

Multitrack targeting is the ability to pursue a number of different targets at the same time without having the concerns related to any of the targets spill over into the pursuit of another. It means being able to separate, within reason, the targets you pursue at work from the targets you pursue with your family. It means being able to focus in on one target at a time, even though your life may be made up of a multitude of targets. It means preventing something I call *target contamination.*

Target contamination means pretty much what it says: It occurs any time your efforts to pursue one target are interfered with or sabotaged by concerns and factors relating to a *different* target (or targets).

You go out to play a round of golf on a Sunday but are so preoccupied with a meeting you have the next day at work that you can't concentrate on your shots. Target contamination. You have a bad day at work and you become unnecessarily and unjustifiably critical of your children at the dinner table. Target contamination. The thoughts of the vacation trip you have planned next month keep interfering with your ability to focus on what's going on at an important business meeting. Target contamination.

Obviously, it's impossible to eliminate target contamination completely from your life. Our brains are not like food processors that can shift gears from chopping to mashing to puréeing at the flick of a switch. If you're facing a thorny situation at work, it's only natural that the worry about the situation is going to weigh on your mind to some degree at

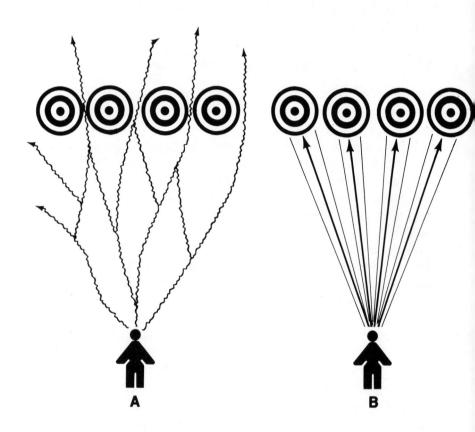

Multitrack targeting is a technique for dealing with a situation in which multiple targets conflict and compete with each other (*A*), creating confusion and giving rise to ineffectual action. The strategy involves setting up separate tracks (*B*) to insulate the targets from each other, so that they can be dealt with one at a time. It is one possible antidote to target contamination.

home. And if you've got a serious problem at home—a sick child, for instance—no reasonable person could expect you to keep your concerns about your child from spilling over to your work. Total compartmentalization is an unrealistic target.

So in particular circumstances and at infrequent times, target contamination is nothing to worry about. The problem only becomes worthy of concern when the contamination is a more or less constant feature in your life. If you go to a concert, you should be able to enjoy the music and not have your mind dwell for half the evening on what you have to do at work the rest of the week. If you go bowling, you should be able to concentrate on the bowling and not be preoccupied with the poor report card one of your children brought home from school. When you're working, you think primarily about work, and when you're at play, you should be thinking about play.

Not that it's easy to do. For target contamination isn't something you deliberately bring upon yourself. It generally occurs *in spite of* your efforts to prevent it. On Friday evening you vow not to give a moment's thought to your job all weekend, yet here it is Saturday afternoon and all you've done all day is think about the job. You *try* not to think about work, but nothing you do—no conversation, no activity, no book—seems to hold your attention for more than a moment or so.

How do you deal with a phenomenon over which you seem to have no control? How do you develop the ability to focus on one target at a time, concentrating on *its* individual requirements, separate from any other target? How, in short, do you develop a "multitrack targeting" approach to life?

Multitrack targeting is not a skill you can develop overnight. You have to cultivate the ability, just as you would cultivate any skill. But the key to developing it is very much tied to how you schedule yourself. The more multitargeted your

life is, the more important it is that your life be fairly well organized—organized according to a multitrack schedule.

The Keys to Multitrack Scheduling

The schedules that each of us follow naturally differ according to what sort of job we have and what sort of life we lead.
But all well-organized schedules are characterized by a number of important features. The three most important of these
elements are:

1. **Routine.**
2. **Compartmentalization.**
3. **Flexibility.**

ROUTINE

The cornerstone to any well-organized schedule is routine.
And for a very good reason. In a very fundamental way, our
sense of well-being is dependent on routine.

Routine benefits us both physically and mentally. Few of
us function at key efficiency when we are forced to make
abrupt changes in our eating or sleeping patterns. Athletes, in
particular, are sensitive to such disruptions. Some athletes
make a fetish of preparing for each new game or match the
same way every time. Jack Kramer, the former tennis champion, did his best to prepare for every big match in exactly
the same way. He always went to bed at the same time, woke
up at the same time, and ate his breakfast at the same time
before an important match.

The impact of the disruption of routine in probably familiar to you if you do a lot of long-distance traveling. Travel,
pleasant though it may be, disrupts our basic biological
rhythms. Insomnia, constipation, fatigue—these are all common symptoms among people who must lead lives which pre-
same time every day. Make your calls at more or less the

vent them from maintaining a steady, rhythmic pattern in their daily routine. Our basic biological needs are best dealt with by means of a consistent, regular schedule or routine.

It's clear as well that our *minds* don't function as effectively when our life rhythms are unstable and when we are constantly obliged to adjust to unfamiliar situations. Surprise and spontaneity are essential elements in a satisfying life, but our brains have not yet evolved to the point where we can function effectively amid a steady diet of change and uncertainty—even if, interestingly enough, the changes are all to the good. Indeed, one of the more interesting findings in stress research over the past few years is that *any* major change in routine, no matter whether good or bad, can be stress inducing.

So, the first principle of multitrack scheduling is to build into your schedule a certain measure of routine. A good way to start is to routinize those activities that are a frequent part of your week. Let's say that you want to build some exercise into your daily or weekly schedule. Try to establish a regular time for it each day (or every other day, depending on your needs). Doing this will make it easier for you, first of all, to keep up with the exercise on a day-in, day-out basis. Habits routinely followed are much easier to hold to. More importantly, your body itself responds better to a regular schedule than to an irregular schedule.

The same principle of routine should also apply to your eating and sleeping. As a general rule, if you have a busy schedule, you should try to eat your meals at approximately the same time each day. Try as well to regularize your sleeping habits.

It also makes good sense to routinize as much as possible your daily *responsibilities*—assuming, that is, that there isn't already an externally established routine. Get into the habit of taking care of your correspondence at more or less the same time. Granted, certain kinds of routine can be punishingly boring. I'm assuming, however, that you have the kind of life or job in which the problem is not one of too much routine, but of too much variety which needs some routine imposed on it. The busier you are and the more varied your responsibilities, the more important it is for you to routinize the basic aspects of your life.

Obviously, there is a limit to the degree of routine you can impose on your life, and you don't want to go overboard. The general rule, though, is that the more targets you have in your life, the more advisable it is for you to routinize as many basic aspects of your life as possible.

COMPARTMENTALIZATION

Compartmentalizing your schedule means setting aside specific blocks of time to attend to specific targets. Doing this insulates one target from another and helps to prevent what one executive I know calls the "nickel and dime effect."

"You get nickeled and dimed to death," he explains. "You're trying to get something done and every ten minutes or so someone is asking you this question or that question, or you're answering the phone. None of the problems is major but each time you get away from what you're doing, you have to crank up again."

There are two ways to compartmentalize. One is on the basis of specific targets. The other is on the basis of the kind of actions or thought processes involved in the reaching of several targets.

To illustrate the differences between the two, let's look at how two editors who work for publishing houses like to operate.

Paul is project-oriented. He likes to spend an entire morning working on one manuscript or one project, regardless of what specific tasks have to be done relating to that project. Arlene is different. She likes to spend a morning doing similar tasks that relate to different manuscripts. For instance, she'll spend Wednesday mornings sending out letters and

Thursday afternoon coordinating production schedules regarding several of the books she's working on.

There are no hard-and-fast rules on which type of compartmentalization works best. It depends on your job, on your own temperament, on specific circumstances within your job. It doesn't really matter on what basis you compartmentalize, the important thing is to build some element of compartmentalization into your schedule. The more intelligently you can separate the various activities that make up your day into their own compartments, the easier it will be for you to do what you have to do with a minimal amount of the distractions that produce target contamination. And here again, as with routinization, your need for compartmentalization increases as the targets in your life become more numerous.

THE IMPORTANCE OF "QUIET" PERIODS

The busier your schedule, the more important it is to include in that schedule periods of the day whose chief purpose is to permit your attentive energies to be recharged. If yours is a truly multitrack day, you need "quiet" or "transition" periods so that the mental residue from one activity isn't still with you when you address yourself to a different activity. If you don't provide for these transition periods, the result is a "piling on" effect that eventually clouds your focus and forces you to expend more attentive energy than you normally would in order to stay on one behavioral track.

I myself depend a great deal on quiet periods during the portion of my day when I am seeing patients. I always allow a few minutes between patients to permit the curtain of one act to fall before the next act begins. A moment of quiet in which my attentive energies can be refreshed.

Incorporating into his schedule such quiet times helped Stephen R., an advertising executive, conquer the extreme nervous fatigue that used to hit at the end of each workday.

Stephen was aware that he needed periods of the day in which to unwind, so he got into the practice of playing squash several times a week. The problem was that he usually worked until the last possible moment during the morning and was forced to race at full speed to the club to be on time for his squash court. What was intended to be a relaxing period actually exacerbated his problem of nervous fatigue.

In Stephen's case, a minor adjustment in scheduling helped solve the problem. Instead of waiting until the last minute before leaving his office for the squash club, he stopped taking all calls a good twenty minutes before he had to be at the squash club. He also started leaving his office ten minutes earlier. This meant that he could walk to the club and not be pressured by the clock. By means of this change he was able to enjoy the forty-five minutes of squash he played for its intended purpose: relaxation.

Remember the point I made earlier. It's hard to shift your attention from one subject to another without being affected to some degree by spillover from the previous object of your focus. You must give yourself time between tasks to regain your mental equilibrium. Don't worry about overdoing it. A few minutes of quiet time several times throughout the day will do wonders to conserve your attentive energy.

FLEXIBILITY

In an imperfect world there is no such thing as a "perfect" schedule. No matter how carefully you structure your time, no matter how many variables you take into consideration, no matter how well you routinize the main areas of your life—eating, sleeping, exercise—there is no way you can control everything around you. Inevitably, situations will arise that you don't expect.

This is why flexibility is so important an ingredient in successful scheduling. Flexibility means building into your schedule some margin for the unexpected, some extra time to serve as a kind of "scheduling insurance policy." Two or three weeks may go by when you will have no use for this extra time. But on the one or two occasions a month when you need it, it can mean the difference between an important target reached, or one botched.

I'm not talking here about a great deal of time. For general purposes, around 10 percent of your workday ought to be set aside for the unexpected. If you're an executive it's a good idea to leave yourself a half hour of *unscheduled* time both in the morning and in the afternoon. If nothing comes up during those periods, use the time to relax or read or attend to personal matters.

Another thing I recommend is the setting aside of at least one sizeable chunk of time in your weekly schedule in which you don't schedule anything at all. I myself deliberately leave Sunday free so I can have the opportunity at least once a week to do what I feel like doing at the moment, to be spontaneous. The fact that my time is so well organized during the rest of the week makes this one day of no scheduling an important part of my overall schedule. I enjoy the spontaneity of a Sunday free of anything prearranged. By the time Monday rolls around, I'm ready to resume my regular schedule.

What is important to bear in mind here is that the reason I can be free on Sunday is that the rest of my week is well organized. My mind is not cluttered with worries about work or other things because I have set up a schedule that works for the rest of my time. You can see how a schedule, if it is organized well, can be, not a confining influence, but a *liberating* influence in your life.

Insulating Yourself from Target Contamination

In the Yukon section of Canada are several remote fishing camps where there are no phones, no easy communication at all with the outside world. The principal clients of these camps happen to be some of the country's most prominent business executives. It is not simply to be different or adventurous that these executives choose such isolated places for periodic vacations. Nor are they all so dedicated to fishing per se. The main reason they go is that such places provide these men with an enforced isolation from the rest of the world. Unable to communicate easily with their offices, the men soon realize the disadvantage of allowing themselves to be preoccupied with thoughts about business. They think about fishing instead. And they relax.

Most of us, of course, can't retreat to a remote Yukon fishing camp in order to escape from the pressures of our everyday lives. But there are a number of steps we can take in order to achieve much the same effect. A magazine editor I know of, for instance, has *two* working areas at her office, one which has no phone and is far removed from the main traffic flow of the floor. Most of the time she works out of her regular office, but when she is up against a deadline and cannot afford the usual distractions, she retreats to the other, important insulating herself from the calls and office visits that would normally put her off track.

To take another example, Pauline L. is active in volunteer work and found that her ability to concentrate on her tasks improved dramatically as soon as she stopped doing the paperwork in her kitchen. "I spend too much time there doing other things," she explained, "and I found my mind constantly drifting." By setting up a small work area for herself in a guest room she found the problem eased.

The degree to which it is necessary to insulate your involvement with other activities will depend, naturally, on how susceptible you are to target contamination. Some fortunate people can keep their attention focused on one target in the midst of many distractions. Most people, though, need a certain amount of arranged insulation. You have to know yourself. If you're the sort of person who cannot help but

Target contamination (*A*) occurs when you are confronted with several targets, all of which should be handled
individually. Because the targets seem to overlap and interfere with one another, it becomes difficult to discrimi-
nate them and to deal with them properly. The solution
(*B*): separate the targets, and deal with them separately.

worry about your job even on weekends, it behooves you to find some leisure activity which forces you to concentrate. One of the reasons that tennis has become so popular, I think, is that it forces you to concentrate deeply on the game itself.

Another way you might try to insulate yourself from target contamination is to look at the people you normally socialize with. How many of them are people you see regularly at work? And how often when you are with them on the weekends does the subject inevitably turn to work? Perhaps it's time to seek out different friends—people you won't be able to talk to about work. Remember, the best way to deal with target contamination is to create the kind of environment in which it is *unlikely* to occur. It's not that difficult to do and it becomes easier to do the more you do it.

How to Stretch Your Day

If you were to visit the New York apartment of a certain Nobel Laureate biologist at 5 A.M. on a typical day, you would probably find him at work in his study. You might reasonably assume he was an insomniac, but you'd be wrong. Like many successful and busy people, this biologist has arranged his schedule so that he can put in two hours of work each morning *before* he goes to his laboratory. If it weren't for that early morning period of reading, working, and reflecting, he doubts that he could ever have made the discoveries that led to his Nobel Prize.

Am I recommending that you, too, consider the possibility of starting your day at 4:30 A.M.? Hardly. On the other hand, if your schedule is such that you can't seem to find enough hours in the day to accomplish everything you want to accomplish and if you're convinced there's no way you can cut down on your target load, your only sensible recourse is to figure out a way to stretch your day.

Let me quickly define what I mean by "stretching" your day. It means increasing the number of hours you are productive. Most people's approach to this problem is to extend their workday: to work longer at the office, or to bring work home. But there are more effective ways of stretching your day.

GETTING AN EARLIER START

Probably the easiest and most sensible way of stretching your day is to wake up an hour or so earlier than you normally do, like the Nobel Prize winner. No grimaces, please. You probably need less sleep than you think. If the idea of getting up an hour or so earlier each day is repugnant to you, it's probably because you have trouble enough getting up at your normal time. But I suspect that if you start your day earlier than you're now starting it and if you use that hour productively, it won't be too long before it is actually *easier* for you to get up in the morning, even if you are getting up earlier.

How can this be? Well, for one thing, sleep needs are governed by both mental and physical fatigue. This is why most of us get along with less sleep when we're on vacation, even though we're more physically active than we normally are. The reason it is so difficult for you to get up each morning (if it is a problem for you) may be that you're still feeling the residual effects of the tensions of the day before. Getting up an hour earlier stretches your day, giving you more time and taking the "rushing" aspect out of the day. The result? Reduced tension. Reduced tension means you'll need less sleep and won't find it nearly as difficult to wake up each morning. It may sound a little Catch-22ish, but the principle is sound. Up to a certain point, you can actually reduce the amount of sleep you need by simply sleeping less.

You may wonder why you can't achieve the same ends by staying up an hour later at night. Some people can do this but most of us can't. The reason should be obvious enough. Most of us are fairly fatigued toward the end of the day. We need to relax, not to work more. And even when we do sit down to some work at night, we are generally not as productive as we are early in the morning, when we're fresh. Exceptions to this rule are of course those "night people" whose available energy is lower in the morning than at night.

If you decide to try getting up an hour earlier, exactly how you choose to spend that extra hour each morning will depend, of course, on the sort of job you have. I know some people who like to use this quiet morning time to plan their day or to think about decisions they have to make. They find they have a clearer perspective when they're away from the office than when they're in the actual job situation. Generally speaking, this quiet period, when you're usually by yourself and don't have to deal with phone calls or other interruptions, is an excellent time for problem solving, for thinking about some of the longer-range aspects of your job that you don't get a chance to consider at the office.

If you have the kind of job in which you're limited in what you can do at home (although it's the rare job that doesn't lend itself to some away-from-the-job thinking), you can still put that extra hour to the pursuit of other targets that are important to your life. I know a woman who gets up at 5:30 A.M. every day just so she can have time to read. She enjoys reading but finds that at night, after work, she doesn't have the energy to concentrate on a book.

There are many other ways the early morning can be put to use. Several doctors I know get up early each day so that they can have a quiet hour in which to review the latest medical literature. Recently I heard of a young computer programmer who taught himself Spanish in three months just by setting aside half an hour each morning before he went to work. Jogging, reading, yoga, meditation, writing letters, doing paperwork—there are any number of things you can get done in that extra hour you give yourself each morning. Even if you do nothing else but soak in a tub and simply relax for a half hour, you'll be helping yourself begin each day on a positive note.

Try it. Tomorrow set your alarm clock fifteen minutes earlier than usual, and use the little bit of extra time to do something you would normally try to work into your schedule. Or use the time to give yourself more time to get started. The next day, increase the time to a half hour and then try getting up an hour earlier. An hour a day may not seem like much, but over a year it adds up to two full weeks. And over an average lifetime, it adds up to more than three years!

Exercise and Diet

Most of the kind of work we do these days is more tiring mentally than physically. Too often we turn to artificial means, like coffee, cigarettes, alcohol, and drugs to keep going. There are better ways, the most important of which is exercise.

Some people may still be under the impression that exercise is excessively tiring. To the contrary, a reasonable amount of exercise actually adds to your energy levels—especially if you have a sedentary job. There is as yet no hard scientific evidence to document it, but it's safe to say that fifteen or twenty minutes of exercise each day, whether it's running or calisthenics, will increase your mental productivity.

Here is an experiment you can try that should prove the point. The next time you're working at home or at the office and you feel yourself getting drowsy, don't reach for a cigarette, don't go to the coffeepot, and don't look for a place to lie down. Instead, go outside and take a brisk walk. Or do about five minutes of rigorous calisthenics. Get your heartbeat going. Then take a couple of minutes to relax before going back to what you were doing when you felt drowsy in the first place. The difference in how you feel will astound you.

I may be biased and overly evangelistic about the benefits of exercise, but I know what it does for me and I see what it has done for many people I know. Forgetting for the moment its long-range benefits for the cardiovascular system, regular exercise can keep up your energy level throughout the day. It helps make you alert and better able to deal with potentially stressful situations. Exercise, in fact, is one of the best day "stretchers" you'll ever find. Even thirty seconds of simple stretching itself can help you get back to your task with greater vigor.

Like exercise, the kind of food you eat goes a long way to affect your energy levels, and in turn the ease or difficulty with which you are able to reach your targets. Unless you're highly unusual, nothing could be worse for your energy level than a heavy noontime meal, especially if it's washed down with generous amounts of alcohol. More and more people realize this and as a result are conducting less and less business at lunch.

Not that you should overlook lunch. But if you've got a busy day, lay off the heavy foods. Stick to salads and vegetables and limit your alcohol. Save the glass of wine for dinner.

Taking Control of Yourself

I have spent very little time in this chapter discussing the specifics of scheduling—that is, how much time you should devote to work, family, leisure, etc. I've done it for a simple reason: I don't think it is my place to dictate how you should apportion your own time.

What I've tried to do instead is to emphasize the possibilities that lie in this frequently overlooked area of scheduling. Regardless of how you want to spend your time, you'll be able to spend it better and more productively if you take steps to put it more under your control. Taking these steps requires no special skills and no special training. You already have a pretty good idea of what you have to do and what you like to do, and you should have an idea of how you function at various times of the day or week. All you have to do now is put the two together. And nobody is in a better position to do it for you than yourself.

TARGET PRACTICE 5

Setting Up a Daily Time Log

The busier you are, the more precious each moment in your day becomes. Yet it's surprising how much time in the day of a "busy" person is simply wasted. An excellent way to see how efficiently you utilize the time in a typical day is to keep a detailed time log for two or three days.

Be as precise as you possibly can. In fact, set up a time log beforehand, divided into ten-minute segments so that all you have to do throughout the course of a day is to write in the activity. The best way to make sure that the log you keep is accurate is to keep it on your desk (or, if you're out of the office, in your pocket or purse) and make your notes at least two or three times an hour. At the end of the day, total up the number of minutes in which you were involved in activity that you would describe as productive. Then compare this total to the number of hours you actually *want* to be productive—that is, the amount of time you spend at work minus any time spent for lunch or specifically planned recreation.

Ideally, you should keep such a log for three different days, randomly spaced over a two-week period. Then, by combining your totals from all three days you can get a fairly accurate picture of your own productivity rate. Anything above ninety percent is very good, but if your ratio of "productive" moments to total moments spent at work is much less, it's probably time to re-examine your work schedule or, better, your work habits.

CHAPTER 6

Target Sweetening:
How to Get Around to
Doing the Things You
Don't Like to Do

If all the targets in our lives were pleasurable to pursue and easy to reach, targeting itself would present few problems. We could set about our tasks with an easy mind and a cheerful spirit. Chances are we wouldn't constantly find ourselves coming up with reasons why we can't or even shouldn't do a particular thing at a particular time. Undoubtedly, we would not be plagued by feelings of guilt or irritation when we fail to get things accomplished.

Unfortunately, however, life affords few of us this easy passage. Regardless of who we are or what we do for a living, it is a safe bet that there are some targets in our lives that, given a choice, we would not pursue. Alas, we are all frequently confronted with targets that bring little or no pleasure, and may even be painful to reach. These are what I call *negative targets*.

A negative target can take any number of forms and will, of course, vary from individual to individual. What may be a truly "negative" target for you may not be a "negative" target for me. For the truth is, the target itself is not generally what is painful or unpleasant. It is our perception of the target, the way we relate to the target, which causes us the trouble.

Making a weekly visit to the home of a close relative is something you might look forward to each week—therefore, a positive target. But for someone else, such a weekly visit might seem a negative target.

Obviously, a target is "negative" less because of *what* it is than because of how we *feel* about it. Doing the laundry, cleaning house, handling reports at work, attending meetings—none of these activities is inherently pleasurable. But the degree to which they are negative varies considerably from person to person and, generally speaking, the more "negative" we find a target, the harder it is for us to deal with that target in a positive, systematic way.

There are always exceptions to this rule. Some people—we sometimes label them "martyrs" or "gluttons for punishment"—go out of their way to surround themselves with negative targets. A dentist I know is forever complaining about how little free time he has. Yet, he is the first person to volunteer whenever an organization he belongs to has a thankless task nobody else will take on. In fact, he deals with them in a very successful manner.

Obviously, people like my dentist friend have their reasons for behaving this way—reasons which are a subject unto themselves and need not really concern us. What concerns me here are those people who fall into the other extreme—those for whom negative targets are a more or less *constant* affliction in life. All of us have a natural tendency to procrastinate when it comes to things we don't really want to do, but the tendency doesn't hurt us all equally. It is one thing, for example, to be a week or two late when it comes to paying monthly bills, but it is something else to get so far behind in payments that you end up paying hundreds of dollars in interest at the end of the year even though you had the money to pay the bill on time. It is one thing to put off for a couple of days having the front tire on the car checked, but something else again to keep putting it off until you find yourself stranded on the highway during rush hour with a flat. It is one thing to postpone making an apology that needs to be made, but something else again to wait so long that a simple apology will no longer be sufficient to patch up a disagreement you may have had with a friend or relative.

The consequences of such behavior can be serious, damaging both to others and to ourselves. Since we all have to deal with negative targets from time to time, we have to learn to deal with them successfully. And we can. You may be the sort of person who can pursue and reach these targets with a fair amount of ease. But if you are a person who has trouble dealing with negative targets frequently, and as a result experience a good deal of inconvenience and unpleasantness because of this tendency, there is a technique that can help you. I call it *target sweetening.*

How to Sweeten the Target

The central idea behind target sweetening is simple. You sweeten a target by making a change that makes it less objectionable, and therefore easier to attend to.

By making a target easier to attend to, I do not mean changing the actual target in any way. What you do is change aspects of the target to make it more appealing.

The steps necessary to effect this change fall into three categories:

1. **Reduce, where possible, the nonessential, negative aspects of the target—that is, the negative aspects that are not an absolutely essential element of the target.**

2. **Cultivate (again, where possible) the positive elements that may exist within a negative target situation, which so far you have failed to recognize or take advantage of.**

3. **Introduce a positive element into the negative target situation—an element that does not materially affect the target itself, but does affect your attitude toward the target.**

A word of caution before going into these concepts in further detail. You will frequently face negative targets that do

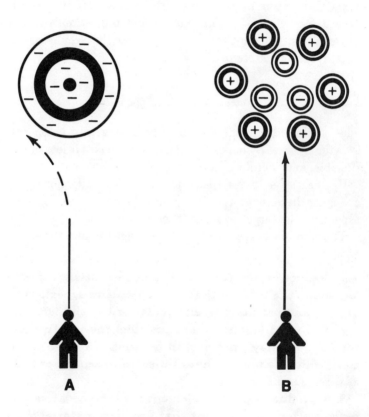

Target sweetening is a way of dealing with a target that has strong negative elements (*A*). The solution (*B*) is to make the target more attractive by adding positive elements and isolating the negative component.

not lend themselves to sweetening. Sometimes you have no alternative but to face up to a specific situation and do what has to be done. On the other hand, there is a good chance that many of the negative target situations in your life can be made a good deal less negative through the use of one or more of the sweetening techniques I've just listed. The techniques work, even if not equally well in every situation. You have to learn when—and how—to apply each of them. Let us take a closer look.

REDUCING THE NEGATIVE

Frequently the things we find most unpleasant about negative targets turn out, upon close investigation, not to be really essential elements of the target. They can be eliminated, or at least considerably reduced in importance.

Maureen was a young woman in her late twenties who thoroughly despised doing the family laundry. It's difficult to fault anybody for not relishing laundry chores, but in Maureen's case doing the laundry had become a real problem for her. She couldn't afford to pay someone to do the laundry for her and she didn't live close to a laundromat. Her children were too young to do their own laundry, and her husband, who was something of a male chauvinist, refused to do it, although he was quick to complain when he ran out of clean underwear. Maureen sometimes let two and three weeks go by before she did the laundry, creating a considerable amount of tension in the home. She was unhappy, her family was unhappy, it was a bad situation.

What can you do in a situation where your distaste for an activity is so intense you simply can't get yourself to do it at all?

What Maureen did, first of all, was to analyze her situation. Doing so brought her to the realization that it wasn't so much doing the laundry she hated, it was spending time in a dingy, spider-infested section of the basement where the washer and dryer happened to be located. She did something about it. She gave the area a paint job. She also had some new light fixtures put in, hung up a couple of inexpensive posters on the walls, and bought a cheap radio to keep there permanently to help distract her from the boring chore. Maureen still isn't crazy about doing the laundry, but she no longer dreads the chore as much as she used to, and it isn't as hard for her to do it now on a fairly regular basis. By eliminating the negative aspects of a situation that were not an essential part of the target task, she sweetened the target and made it that much easier to attend to.

Are there unessential negative aspects of negative targets in your own life that you might be able to do away with? There is an easy enough way to find out. Start by analyzing the overall situation, the "target environment."

Break the negative target down into as many parts as you can.

Consider the location—where you have to pursue the target. Is that part of the problem? Consider the people you must come into contact with.

Think about the specific dynamics of the target—what you actually have to do in order to reach the target. Think about when you have to do the task.

Once you've brought to the surface some of the negative features surrounding the target, ask yourself these questions:

1. Which of these features is objectionable to me?
2. Is this feature an absolutely essential ingredient in the target-reaching process?

In all likelihood, you will uncover a negative feature that is not essential to the target itself. You are now in a position to think about modifying this feature. You might even be able to do away with this feature entirely. Not *every* negative target, upon closer investigation, will yield up these nonessential and objectionable features, but a close examination of the elements which surround a target may be a very useful and surprising exercise. Target sweetening is much more than a simple mental trick; it is much more than just starting to see a half-empty glass as a half-filled glass. It is a careful analysis and consideration of the specific elements which surround a seemingly negative target.

Consider Phil K., an executive in an electronics company. Phil is one of those people who genuinely loathes doing paperwork. He considers it an irritating interruption of the constructive and creative work he does. But when he performed the analytical exercise I've just described, he discovered that one of the most negative aspects of his overall target was that he was always under severe pressure to get the reports in on time. It wasn't only the collating of information and the preparing of the reports that Phil found so difficult to deal with, it was the *pressure* he felt when he finally got around to writing them up.

Phil took a simple step—one of those steps so simple that he wondered, as we all do from time to time, why he had never taken it before. He drew up a schedule which provided him time to get started on the reports a few days earlier in the month. Even more important, he designed the schedule so that he never had to spend more than an hour at a time working on them. Soon he found the pressure was off and, even better, he discovered that since he had limited the amount of time he spent on the paperwork each time, the target became far more palatable and therefore easier to approach.

There are a number of other examples I can cite to illustrate the same concept of target sweetening. Henry P., a pilot, discovered that the yard work he found terribly unpleasant to do and often put off for weeks, wasn't nearly as disagreeable if he got up early and did the work before it got too hot. It wasn't the work itself he disliked so much; it was the discomfort of working in the hot sun. Once this negative—and, in Henry's case, nonessential—ingredient was done away with, the target itself no longer seemed negative.

To reiterate what I mentioned earlier, not every negative target has ingredients that can be eliminated without changing the nature of the target itself. Even in those targets where it is possible to isolate negative ingredients not directly related to the target, it isn't always possible or convenient to make changes. But if you take a good, hard look at the negative targets in your life, if you analyze them and break them down so that you can discover just what is objectionable to you about the target, and/or its environment, chances are good you'll discover in more cases than you might expect that you're subjecting yourself to unpleasantness that is not only unnecessary, but counterproductive as well.

CULTIVATING POSITIVE INGREDIENTS

The second concept often useful in target sweetening is cultivating the positive ingredients in what is originally seen as a negative target.

Once a week, for six years, Marilyn P. used to visit her mother in a nursing home. Marilyn's mother was bedridden and barely able to carry on a coherent conversation, and it wasn't long before the mere thought of the visit was enough to make Marilyn depressed. Many of us should be able to identify with Marilyn's situation, for we've had similar experiences. Marilyn, however, reacted to her situation in an interesting and enterprising way, a way neatly illustrating the principle of how to cultivate the positive aspects of a negative target.

Marilyn realized there was little she could do to alter in any fundamental way the negative aspects of the visits. She was saddened and depressed by her mother's state. She also felt the visits were rather pointless since her mother hardly recognized her. Nevertheless, it occurred to her that as long as she had to go to the home anyway, why not do something useful and spend a couple of extra hours helping out?

Through her volunteer work at the nursing home, she became friendly with other people who had parents in the home. She also came to know the staff at the nursing home much better. She and one of the nurses, in fact, got into the habit of exchanging homebaked breads each week. The result: The negative aspects of visiting a bedridden, nearly senile parent every week remained the same, but the ancillary aspects of the experience were positive enough to make Marilyn actually look forward to her weekly visit.

To be sure, there is always a danger of overdoing it when trying to cultivate positive elements in negative target situations. The danger is in expending so much energy in the effort to eliminate the negative that the entire exercise becomes counterproductive. An example of what I'm talking about are people who become so preoccupied with being "comfortable" on a backpacking trip that they end up with a backpack so packed with goods they wear themselves out carrying it.

Then, too, it is probably more difficult to cultivate the positive aspects of a negative situation than it is to reduce or eliminate negative aspects which exist within the situation. Certainly it's more of a challenge. The challenge is to recognize the possibility of positive elements and identify them in these targets. I'm not talking here about simply changing your point of view—looking for the proverbial silver lining. I'm talking about recognizing *real* positive possibilities in negative situations.

The possibilities are generally there, if you look for them. As bizarre as it may seem, I know a woman who has actually learned to enjoy housework now that she has started to combine a physical fitness workout with the housecleaning routine. She has six rooms to dust and vacuum, and she has de-

vised a sequence of calisthenics that calls for a certain
number of exercises to be done in each room. In this way, she
uses the time within the negative target situation to positive
effect.

The same concept is also exemplified by commuters who
don't like the train or bus trip they have to make each day
but make the best of a poor situation by reading or doing
work. I know a psychologist who wrote a book one year during the two hours a day he spent on the train commuting to
New York City.

More than anything you need to confront a negative situation with an open mind. You have to be willing to look beyond the obvious, to cultivate the positive elements of a situation. Are you often compelled to spend time with people you
find difficult to converse with or think boring? Rather than
dismissing such people as out and out "bores," see if you can
find a topic you share an interest in, whether it is food, children, home carpentry, cars, sports, travel—anything.

Is there a trip you have to make frequently that you find
more difficult to make each time? Try varying the route you
take. Sample different restaurants on the way. Do you find a
class you have to attend stifling and boring? Instead of sur-
rendering to boredom, try to *transcend* the boredom by cultivating a deeper interest in the subject. Instead of saying, "I
hate history, it's my worst subject, it's boring," spend a few
days trying to gain a better understanding of the subject. It
may well be that the boredom lies more with you than in the
subject.

No example I can think of better illustrates the target
sweetening possibilities of cultivating the positive than one
involving a married couple I know. The wife had been a music
major in college and loved opera. Her husband had always
thought he had a "tin ear." He couldn't be bothered with opera. It bored him. To please his wife, the husband would go to
the opera occasionally but always with reluctance and always

with his mind miles away. Then the couple met and became friendly with a man who directed opera, a lively, entertaining person whose company the husband enjoyed. At the director's prodding, the husband began to listen to more opera at home and even went to a couple of rehearsals. You can guess what happened. Today, the husband is an even bigger opera buff than his wife.

There's no need to belabor the point. While there are limits in applying the principle of cultivating positive elements in negative situations, the least you can do is to stay open to them, to be on the lookout for the positive elements that are almost always present in every situation, waiting to be cultivated by the energetic seeker.

Introducing the Positive into the Target

If a negative target lends itself to neither a reduction in its negative elements nor a cultivation of its positive elements, there is still a third sweetening possibility: introducing a positive target into the negative situation. Conceptually, there is a similarity between cultivating the positive elements already existing in a situation and introducing new, positive elements into the situation. In both cases you are establishing positive targets. The difference is that in this third technique of target sweetening you're bringing something *new* into the target situation, something that wasn't there before.

Here's an example.

Donald P. is a commercial artist who throughout his adult life has always found it inordinately difficult to pay his bills regularly and keep his checkbook balanced every month. He hates, simply hates, the idea of sitting down for two or three hours every month to get his financial affairs in good order. Were Donald a rich man, he could hire an accountant to handle all his finances, but he cannot afford that expense. He has taken another approach. Each month he waits until there is a sporting event on television he knows he'll enjoy watching. And he schedules his bill-paying time for that particular time segment. (By now, I hope you have noticed that scheduling is an essential tool in target sweetening.)

Here again, let me emphasize the fine line between the practical application of a target-sweetening technique and the impractical application of it. You might argue that a man like Donald would be better off if he simply "grew up" and resigned himself to the fact that once a month he has to set aside a few hours for his finances. But the reality of the situation is that Donald *can't* do this. In the past his inability to manage his money has caused him a tremendous amount of inconvenience, what with his phone being disconnected, checks bouncing, credit being refused. He has found a practical solution to his problem, and even though he's taking a contrived action, it works. The bills get paid. His checkbook gets balanced. Whatever works for you is what you should do. You may have to try several techniques before you find the right answer to your particular needs.

Let's look at another example.

Betty R. and Jean C. are two suburban women who find marketing an unpleasant chore and therefore a negative target. To make the target less negative they decided to do their marketing together. Once or twice a week they go to the store, help one another unload the grocery bags, and finish off by having lunch together. They have introduced a positive target—spending time with a close friend—into a negative target situation—food shopping—with productive results.

Many parents, of course, routinely use this principle of target sweetening in dealing with their children. A child dreading a visit to the dentist is promised an ice-cream cone or a toy if he willingly goes. Call it a bribe, if you want, but a positive element has been introduced into a negative situation.

(There's nothing wrong with rewarding positive action.) It's only surprising that so few parents ever utilize the same principle in their own lives. Let's say that Thursday is an especially harried day for you. Why not build into Thursday evening something positive: a dinner out, a tennis game, or a movie? Give yourself the same reward or break you would give to somebody else if you wanted to sweeten the target they must pursue.

The technique of target sweetening can also be used to add appeal to routine tasks in your workday that you may now have problems attending to. I know of two executives, a president of a tobacco company and his executive vice-president, who used target sweetening very cleverly. They both felt it important to visit personally a section of the main plant every day. To make the target more appealing, the men had a standing bet to see which of them could call more of the employees by name. This added bit of competition made a "game" out of what could have been a routine part of each man's day. Incidentally, it also did wonders for the morale of the workers in the company.

Try the concept yourself. See if you can make a game out of the mundane, everyday tasks in your life. Set time goals for yourself. If it took you forty-five minutes to finish a routine task yesterday, see if you can do it in forty minutes today. Offer yourself a reward if you meet the target—a longer work break, for instance. Here, too, don't be afraid to experiment. Keep in mind that it is never the task or the target itself that is boring, it is the perception you have of it and the way you relate to it. Change the environment of the target, sweeten it up, and you can often change the perception.

A Final Look at Target Sweetening

Target sweetening is a technique designed to make some of the negative targets in your life easier to confront and therefore easier to reach. As I've said several times, target sweetening does not always lend itself equally well to all situations. There will even be some situations where it doesn't work at all. The question of when target sweetening is practical and useful and when it isn't is something only you can answer. My personal feeling is that the technique should be explored—and used—primarily in situations where the negative aspects of a target are causing you noticeable and measurable difficulty. Examine the whole of these situations with an open mind, and don't be afraid to experiment. There is no law that says routine chores must be boring, no law that says obligatory social functions must be unpleasant for you. You can have some control, even in these situations. Certainly there is a balance point beyond which the energy you invest in target sweetening may be wasted energy, but in most cases you will be able to tell easily enough when this point has been passed. In the meantime, not to reach this point is to do yourself an unnecessary injustice.

TARGET PRACTICE 6

Techniques of Target Sweetening

Target sweetening is more than a mental exercise in which you "talk" yourself into thinking things are better than they really are. It involves specific steps you can take to make negative targets more appealing and therefore easier to pursue. Here are two suggestions to help you get started.

1. Think of somebody other than yourself who is faced with what you would consider a negative target. Now think of some of the ways you would sweeten this negative target. By using somebody else as a subject, you give yourself additional perspective. Once you see it's possible with somebody else, you're more likely to try the techniques on yourself with a more open mind.

2. Get used to the idea of viewing negative targets not as "things you don't like to do," but rather as targets that have negative elements. By viewing targets in this way, you create a mental environment more conducive to the kind of changes you need to make to give negative targets more appeal.

CHAPTER 7

The Diversionary Target Trap and How to Avoid It

In the late 1950s there was a popular movie called *The Hustler*. It starred Paul Newman as an expert pool player who made his living duping lesser players into thinking he was no more skilled at the game than they were, the better to lure them into money games.

As the movie makes clear, one of the things a pool hustler has to be careful about is looking *too* good—even when he wins. A pool hustler's target, in other words, isn't merely to win but to conceal the fact that he's actually a great pool player.

Newman's character was well aware of this danger, but in one scene he loses his cool and takes exception to some derogatory remarks being made by the other players. Forgetting his real target, he decides to "show these guys how the game is really supposed to be played." In the process, he gives away his identity. The other players show their appreciation in a painful way: They break the hustler's thumbs. The hustler has been victimized by something I choose to call a *diversionary target*.

What Is a Diversionary Target?

A diversionary target is any target that draws your behavioral focus away from your primary target. In some instances it can actually sabotage your efforts to reach your primary target.

Often, of course, such a switch in focus happens legitimately and out of necessity. For example, say you're in the middle of baking a cake when the baby falls off a kitchen stool. If you run to take care of the child, you will pretty much ruin your chances of turning out a good cake. The priorities in this case, however, are obvious. Taking care of your baby—the diversionary target—is clearly much more important than the cake. The choice you make to shift from your original target to that diversionary target is entirely proper under the circumstances.

My concern in this chapter is with diversionary targets that do not reflect an understanding of priorities and do not reflect an intelligent choice—those targeting situations in which the shift in focus from a primary target to the diversionary target happens out of anger or fear or a lack of concentration—or because of some other emotional reaction. I am talking about those situations in which you have a clear idea of *what* you have to accomplish and *how* to accomplish it, but find that your behavioral focus goes astray. Because of some interferences, you allow yourself to be diverted from your original target for a diversionary target.

The following hypothetical conversation between a father and his teenage son illustrates what I mean. The father has just received word from his son's advisor at school that the boy is goofing off in class and failing most of his subjects. The father's target is to impress upon his son the importance of changing his ways.

FATHER: Bill, I want to talk to you about school.

BILL: Dad, I really don't want to talk about school.

FATHER: What do you mean, you don't want to talk about school? School is very important. That's your problem. You never want to discuss anything that's important.

BILL: That's not true.

FATHER: It is, too, true. Last week I wanted to talk to you about your driving, and you didn't want to talk then either.

BILL: I had a good reason. There's nothing wrong with the way I

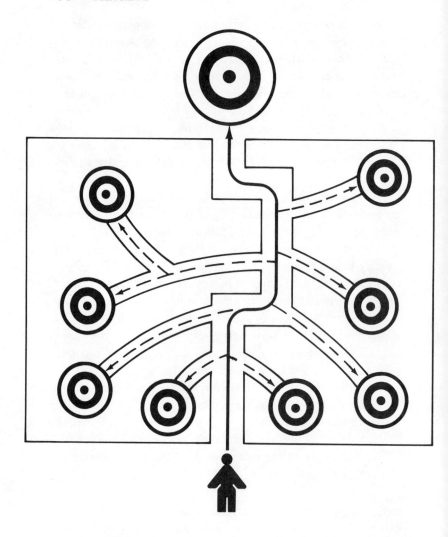

Diversionary targets are minor targets that create distractions, that draw attention from the main business at hand.
It takes considerable concentration to be able to keep on
track to a main target. Being alert to the possibility of diversionary targets helps keep you on the right track.

drive a car. I've never had any accidents. *You* drive worse than I do.

FATHER: How in the world can you sit there and say that you drive better than I do? I've been driving for twenty-five years, and you've only been driving for one year. You're much more careless than I am . . .

Let's stop the dialogue right here. You can see what is happening. The father's primary original target—getting Bill to change his behavior in school—has been pushed aside. As we left the conversation, the father has shifted his focus to an entirely unrelated and diversionary target: that of convincing his son that he, the father, is a better driver.

Had the father deliberately shifted targets as part of an overall strategy to reach his primary target, the hypothetical conversation above would not serve as a negative example of diversionary targeting. But this particular shift in focus has happened without the father's conscious awareness. Something the boy said has triggered a counterproductive reaction, a reaction of anger and pride in the father in much the same way as the insults from the pool players triggered the ill-considered reaction from the pool hustler in the movie.

Here's another example of the same phenomenon. It is 3:30, Friday afternoon, at your office. You're anxious to get an early start for the weekend, but you still have to put the finishing touches on a sales report. Your assistant has been supplying you with the figures you need. In quickly checking over the figures you discover that your assistant has made some mistakes. The following exchange occurs:

YOU: This last set of figures you gave me—there's a mistake here.
ASSISTANT: Are you sure? I'm trying to be careful.
YOU: Well, you're not doing a very good job of it. I can't depend on you anymore. You're not working as hard as you used to.
ASSISTANT: That isn't true.
YOU: No? What about last week when I asked you to doublecheck the spelling of that guy's name from marketing. You still got it wrong.

ASSISTANT: That wasn't my fault. His secretary gave me that spelling over the phone.

YOU: Come on! Do you expect me to believe that a man's secretary would misspell the guy's name over the phone. You *heard* wrong. Maybe you should get your ears checked.

Here, again, it is not necessary to go any further. It's obvious what's happened. Your primary target, in case you've forgotten, was to get the report finished so you could leave the office early. But look where you're headed now—going off in a very different direction. Your new, diversionary target has now become to get your assistant to recognize the folly of his—or her—ways. Whether or not you are justified in your criticism of him is not important under the circumstances. Even if you are successful in achieving this diversionary target, it certainly isn't going to bring you any closer to your primary target of getting the report done so you can leave early. Indeed, your efforts to reach this diversionary target might well end up sabotaging your efforts to reach your primary target. It's possible, for instance, that you could so alienate your assistant, the assistant might decide to walk out, leaving you with the whole job to do.

In each of the situations just mentioned, the same pattern is at work. The target is clearly defined, but something intervenes to pull your eye and your attention away from the original target. In neither of these situations could that particular something have been prevented from appearing. What could have been prevented, however, was the reaction which led you to switch your focus from the primary target to the diversionary target.

It is an extremely important point, one which bears repeating. Preventing diversionary targets from popping up every now and then is all but impossible. Assistants make mistakes. Children say things that have no basis in fact. Pool players make derogatory comments. But if you are not to fall victim

time and time again to diversionary targets, you have to cultivate a discipline that will do two things for you:

1. Increase your awareness of diversionary targets.
2. Keep your focus on the primary target, regardless of the diversionary targets that vie for your attention.

Throughout the rest of this chapter, we will look at some of
the techniques that can help you develop the mental skills
needed to cultivate and utilize this discipline.

Keeping Your Eye on the Target

As any athlete who competes in a ball sport will tell you, few
principles are more central to success than keeping your eye
on the ball. The same thing holds true for targeting.

Simply put, the more strongly reinforced and the more
clearly defined in your mind's eye your primary target is, the
less likelihood there is that a diversionary target can draw attention away from that primary target. Diversionary targets
may arise and may trigger reactions, but if the image of your
primary target is strong enough and compelling enough, you
should be able to keep your attention fixed on the right behavioral track.

What we're talking about here is maintaining attention,
the ability to concentrate. There are two ways of looking at
what happens when you shift your focus from a primary to a
diversionary target. One way is to say that you've developed a
stronger temporary interest in the diversionary target than
you had in the primary target. The other way is to say that
you've lost interest temporarily in the primary target.

The difference in these two ways of looking at diversionary
targets is nicely illustrated by an observation once made by
the champion tennis player Billie Jean King. One of the constant challenges a tennis player faces is maintaining intense

concentration on the game, and in particular keeping his or her eye on the ball. There are any number of potential distractions (read, diversionary targets) that can lead the player to focus attention on something other than the ball—a game taking place in an adjacent court, a group of children playing along the sideline, a plane flying overhead, a bad call.

Billie Jean King's theory is that the best way to prevent these distractions from disrupting concentration is to take steps *ahead of time* to reinforce the importance of watching the ball. One of the things she recommends to tennis players is that they set aside fifteen or twenty minutes a couple of times a week and do nothing but stare at a tennis ball. "If you can stay interested in a tennis ball by doing nothing else but staring at it for fifteen minutes," Billie Jean King once said, "it will make it that much easier to stay interested in the ball and pay attention to it more in a match. And if you can pay enough attention to the ball in a match, distractions will be less of a problem for you."

This same concept of "mental preparation" can be very successfully applied to many life situations—within reason, of course. I'm not suggesting anything elaborate, complicated, or even very time-consuming. All that's involved is a moment or two of what could best be called "mental rehearsal" preceding the situation you want to focus your attention on.

Imagine, for instance, that you are the father in the situation I described earlier. The target remains the same: You want to talk to your son in such a way that he will take his schoolwork more seriously. But you know from past experience—or *should* know, if you reflect on previous situations—that conversations with your son tend to get off track. This time, however, you're determined to prevent it from happening. What you do is simple: You create in your mind a "rehearsal" of the conversation about to take place. You try to hear yourself framing a reply to his resistance that does not lead to diversionary targeting. Having mentally rehearsed the scene, the conversation that eventually takes place might go like this.

FATHER: Billy, I want to talk with you a little about your schoolwork.

BILLY: Dad, I really don't want to talk about school.

FATHER: I can understand that, and I'm not out to attack you. I just want to talk some things over with you . . .

It would be naive of me to suggest that by engaging in a little bit of mental rehearsal, you will be guaranteed a conversation duplicating the conversation you had beforehand in your mind. Hardly. It is possible that your son may react in a way you never expected, producing from you a reaction you didn't rehearse. Mental rehearsal is not a panacea for avoiding the trap of diversionary targets, but it is a step in the right direction. In certain situations, where past experience has shown a certain predictable pattern, the technique works well. In order for the technique to work, you must be sufficiently sensitive to the dynamics of diversionary targeting in your particular situation. Taking the time to reflect on the elements of the situation, even rehearsing a possible scenario, can do the trick. So that you can mentally anticipate the agents that get you off track. With such a preparation you are much more likely to be able to overcome them.

Let me describe for you how the technique worked for Doris, a woman in her late twenties who, despite her many excellent qualifications, was having a problem getting a good job. "I know what the problem is," Doris told me when we first began to address ourselves to her problem. "I get furious when the job interviewer starts to ask me questions that I know he wouldn't be asking if I were a man. It burns me up. I can't help myself. I have to put the interviewer in his place, and I usually blow the interview."

Here is an obvious case of a diversionary target. Doris' primary target was clear: a good job in a corporation. But every time she found herself in an interview situation, a diversionary target arose: instructing job interviewers about the inequities that women face looking for corporate positions.

In order for Doris to overcome her difficulty, two things had to happen. First, she had to clarify in her mind the *unrelatedness* of the two targets. She had to recognize that by challenging the questions being asked her, she was not only not helping her cause, she was actually hurting it. To Doris, the principle of sexual discrimination was an important one. But her primary target was also important, even crucial to her. So the principle was not at issue here. At issue was getting a job.

Adapting the technique of mental rehearsal, we recreated past interviews Doris had had. One went like this:

INTERVIEWER: Would it create a problem for you at home with your child if you had to travel for a few days?
DORIS: I don't feel that's a fair question.
INTERVIEWER: Why not?
DORIS: You wouldn't ask the same question of a man, would you?

In discussing this interview, we considered Doris' reply in many lights. Did Doris have a right to reply the way she did? In principle, yes, just as Paul Newman in *The Hustler* had a right to show the other pool players how terrific he really was as a pool shark. But was her reply directed successfully toward her primary target of getting a job? No!

The second stage of the mental rehearsal process in Doris' case was to get her to create a similar situation in her mind in which the sensitive question or one very much like it also gets asked. But this time in her rehearsal she is ready for it and it *doesn't* elicit the diversionary targeting reply.

INTERVIEWER: If you had to travel for a few days, would this create a problem for you at home with your two children?
DORIS: Not really. I have excellent and dependable help at home.

Let me stress that Doris is no less bothered by the impropriety of the question in the second dialogue than she was in the first. She has not forsworn her belief in women's rights. The difference, however, is that she has mentally prepared herself for her own reaction to the question and is thus able to overcome her anger and answer in a way more suited to her primary target of getting a job.

In how many situations in your own life do you find yourself time and again getting sidetracked by diversionary targets? To ask the same question another way, how many times do you fail to accomplish what you set out to do because you allow yourself to be diverted away from your primary target—by targets completely unrelated to that primary target?

If the pattern occurs frequently it may be time to take stock of yourself, to take steps that can reduce its negative impact. Here are some steps you can take:

1. **Analyze your situation.** The first thing to do in analyzing your situation is to use visualization. Recall specific examples of how you lost control of the intended target. Replay in your mind the situations in which the diversionary targeting generally occurs. In almost every instance, you will note something that triggered the shift. If you're honest with yourself, you will usually be able to isolate the disruptive agent. It may be a subject you are sensitive about: your weight, your sex, your political convictions, money. Try to retrace the sequence that took place once these sensitive subjects emerged. Try to pinpoint as accurately as possible the exact point at which the diversionary target began to draw your focus away from your primary target.

2. **Use mental rehearsal.** Once you've clarified the dynamics of diversionary targeting as they apply to your particular situation, create in your mind scenes in which the same dynamics occur but do not draw your attention to the diversionary target. *Imagine* something someone said about a subject that gets into your craw and causes you to shift your focus from the primary target to a diversionary one. Try to *feel* the answer that rises, really try to experience the emo-

tion that intervenes. Then think of a new response and write a new script, this time supplying the reaction that will keep you on the track that will take you to your primary target.

Going "With" the Diversion

Up to this point the diversionary targets we've been concerned with have been situational, limited to the situation in which they actually present themselves. They possess little in the way of long-range significance. Occasionally, however, a diversionary target emerges that may not be pressing enough to supplant the primary target but is nonetheless a target that does warrant your attention.

An example: Let's say one day you establish the target of clearing up a huge raft of paperwork that has accumulated over the past two weeks. The reason it's important to clear up this paperwork is that you're going on vacation in a couple of days and can't leave with a clear conscience until the work is done. Going through the mountain of letters and reports, your eye catches a number of spelling mistakes made by your assistant. The errors bother you—enough so that the impulse to have a heart-to-heart chat with your assistant about accuracy emerges strongly as a diversionary target.

Because you realize that now is not the ideal time to discuss the problem with your assistant, you decide to ignore the errors, keeping your concentration focused on your original primary target. But the more you read and the more errors you pick up, the more preoccupied with them you become and the harder it becomes to ignore the diversionary target. What do you do?

TARGET UPGRADING

The strategy I recommend in this situation might be called *target upgrading*. It consists of taking a diversionary target

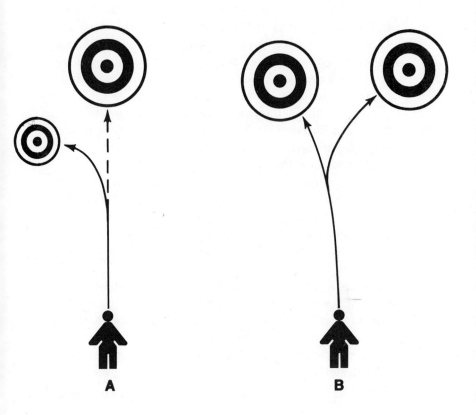

Target upgrading is a way of dealing with a diversionary target (*A*)—one that creates a distraction from a major goal. The strategy involves moving the diversionary target from its attention-getting position and making it a major target (*B*).

and giving it the status of a primary target—although at some future date when it is more practical to pursue it. Don't confuse this technique with procrastination, a subject we'll be looking into later. True procrastination is when you put off timely tasks that demand to be attended to. Target upgrading involves targets in which timing isn't particularly crucial. In the long run, it probably is more important to have an assistant who produces careful, accurately spelled work than it is to finish up a bunch of paperwork so you can go on vacation with a clear desk, but in this case, there's no reason the discussion can't wait until *after* you've come back.

The test of whether an apparently pressing diversionary target can be set aside for the time being is embodied in a very simple question: What will be lost (What will I lose?) by not attending to this target right now?

If the answer to this question is "nothing" or "very little," you can set up the diversionary target as a future, primary target. Take out your calendar. Select a date a few days after you're scheduled to come back from vacation. Block out an hour or two for the specific purpose of having that conversation.

You will benefit in several ways. First, you will remove some of the urgency from the diversionary target, making it easier to deal with later, when you are calm. Also, having settled in your mind that the situation will be dealt with when you come back, the mistakes you find as you read through the reports and letters will no longer bother you or divert your attention as much now, when you are concentrating on getting through the paperwork.

The overall point is that in certain situations where a diversionary target is pressing enough to interfere with your efforts to reach your primary target—and you are consciously aware of what's going on—you don't necessarily have to pursue that diversionary target immediately in order to attend to it. By making a mental commitment to take care of it at some more appropriate time—that is, by targeting—you can greatly minimize the disruptive consequences of the diversion.

As you may have noted by now, this principle applies in particular to family situations. Too many times family occasions that should be free of irritation and tension—meals, vacations, outings—are ruined because parents choose the occasion to "teach the children a lesson." I have children of my own and I don't have to be reminded about the vicissitudes of raising children. But I've learned that there is a time for lessons to be taught and a time to bite the bullet and overlook—for the time being—behavior you don't particularly approve of.

The question to ask yourself in such situations is: *What will I lose by not attending to this target at this moment?*

Say you're at a restaurant and your ten-year-old son isn't the model of good manners that you'd like him to be. Your first impulse is to criticize him and set him straight. If you do, no doubt you may very well cast a pall over the entire meal, destroying everyone's enjoyment—and the enjoyable meal was your original target.

Do you ignore the behavior entirely? Not at all, but you ask yourself the question and you realize that if you wait until you get home before you talk to your son you can treat what is now a diversionary target as a primary target then. By making this decision, by turning a diversionary target into a primary target, but one for a later time, you stay on the track of the target you're pursuing at dinner: a pleasant family outing.

TARGET PRACTICE 7

Handling Diversionary Targets

The first step in the effective handling of diversionary targets is to develop an awareness of them—not as simple a trick as you might think. For starters, tell yourself that over the next three days you're going to become supersensitive to diversionary targets, whether they relate to you or to other people with whom you come into contact. At your next business meeting, for example, allow yourself to become an observer. While you yourself maintain a fix on the primary target, notice how frequently issues arise which have nothing to do with the primary target.

Once you think you've developed sufficient awareness, get into the habit (for at least a week or so) of reviewing in your mind situations in which your target was very clear. In looking over these situations, try to see how many times—if at all—your focus shifted. If you discover a number of focus shifts, try that much harder the next time to maintain a steadier focus.

Be particularly conscious of diversionary targets in family discussions, for this is an area where the problem tends to arise the most. Make a mental note, prior to any discussion, of what it is you want to stay focused on and make a conscious effort to resist any temptation to move away from that target.

CHAPTER 8

Target Obsession: Getting There If It Kills You

How many times has this happened to you? You're about to leave home for a movie or a dinner engagement when you realize you've misplaced your keys. You remember bringing the keys in the house so that you know they're not lost. Anyway, you have a duplicate set in the kitchen drawer so you're not in serious trouble. Common sense also tells you that if you take a few minutes tomorrow, you should be able to find the keys without too much difficulty.

Still and all, not being able to find your keys bothers you. It bothers you so much that finding them suddenly assumes an *exaggerated* importance. So even though you're already running late, and even though there is another set readily at hand, you start searching for them, your anger rising steadily.

Your spouse tries to reason with you, pointing out what you already know—that it will be wiser to look for the keys in the morning. Take the duplicates and get going! But you're not about to listen to reason. It irks you that the keys are missing and so you continue to search for them, getting angrier with each passing moment. Finally, after twenty minutes of frantic searching, you find the keys underneath a magazine in the den. You feel relieved, but the relief is short-lived, because you realize that now you're too late to catch the movie, or embarrassingly late for dinner. Your spouse is furious. You've reached the target you set for yourself—finding the keys—but in the process you've ruined your evening.

I describe the behavior in the above situation as *target obsession*. A target presents itself and you become so blinded in the pursuit of it that you lose the capacity to see clearly, to make sensible judgments.

Target obsession can be a temporary condition, or it can stay with you for days, weeks, and months. The severity of it can vary, too. The condition frequently crops up in family situations, as it did in Florence M.'s case. Florence was a loving, well-meaning parent whose relationship with her fifteen-year-old daughter was deteriorating because of the way in which her daughter took care of (or didn't, according to Florence) her room.

Discussing the situation with Florence made it obvious to me that while her daughter was a little sloppy in her housekeeping habits, she was very nearly a model child. She was sensitive, hard-working in school, and popular among her friends. Florence, however, was so intent on one aspect of her daughter's behavior that she allowed it to blind her and to assume so much importance that it was very nearly destroying their relationship. In her more reasonable moments, Florence herself recognized that the ability to keep a room straight is only one small part of what makes a fifteen-year-old girl tick. Eventually she learned to handle the situation more satisfactorily.

A much more pervasive—and familiar—example of target obsession can be found in the Watergate scandal break-in and cover-up. Nearly everyone connected with the Watergate scandal had more or less the same target: to keep Richard Nixon in the White House. But the target became so paramount in the minds of so many people that it prompted decisions and actions that, in retrospect, were completely misguided.

It was obvious from the polls, for one thing, that Nixon's opponent in the 1972 election, George McGovern, had little chance to beat Nixon. It's also difficult to understand why somebody in authority wasn't aware of the potential consequences of a Watergate break-in. And didn't do his best to stop it. But again, this is precisely what happens when target blindness strikes. Good judgment and reason go out the window. What is obvious to people on the outside looking in is overlooked by people on the inside looking out.

Forgetting for the moment the question of the legality or illegality of the Watergate break-in, the fact remains that in fact it wasn't even necessary as a campaign strategy. The only reason it seemed necessary was that people planning Nixon's reelection were so consumed by their passionate pursuit of their target that they were unable to make reasonable judgments.

Compounding the mistake, even after the scandal broke, the pattern of target obsession persisted, although now the target assumed a new form: keeping the scandal from touching the President. Of all the ironies that characterize the Watergate scandal, none is more striking than the fact that Nixon, the symbol of political pragmatism, the supremely political animal, ordinarily so effective in his target orientation, was so caught up in protecting his flanks that he failed to use the very techniques that had sustained his political career. Indeed, the picture that emerges of Nixon in the final days of his presidency is not that of a cunning fox but of an obsessed man systematically orchestrating his own destruction.

Dissecting Target Obsession

To understand the dynamics of target obsession, we must first differentiate between two types of target-oriented behavior: behavior energized by desire or determination built on a logical basis, and behavior energized by desire or determination based on an illogical and, perhaps, obsessive nature.

Clearly, you can't expect to reach your targets if you aren't determined, or cannot summon the energy needed to pursue them. As Michael Korda notes in his book *Success,* "Desire,

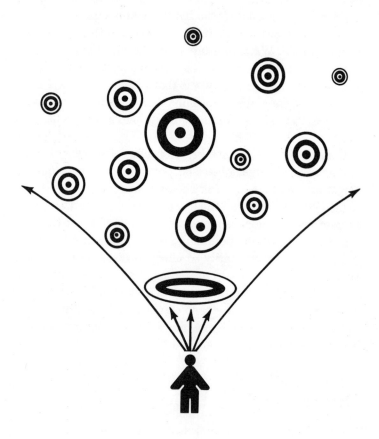

Target obsession is overinvolvement with a secondary and unimportant target to the point where it blocks your view and causes you to lose sight of more important targets. This is applying yourself to one thing to the exclusion of everything else.

determination, a sense of timing are the common denominators of success, of far more importance than any other factors."

But too much desire and too much determination can produce judgments that are clouded and misdirected.

The distinction between not enough energy and/or determination and too much isn't easy to make. The measure of target obsession isn't so much found in the intensity of the desire itself but, rather, the consequences of it. Many successful people bring an enormous amount of desire and determination to a target-oriented task, yet always manage to maintain the perspective needed to make appropriate judgments. For some people even the slightest degree of emotional involvement in a target is enough to produce target blindness. A great many parents are insightful and rational in some areas of their lives, but find it impossible to view their children with any degree of objectivity.

While we're making distinctions, let's differentiate, too, between a target obsession and preoccupation. Many, if not all of us, experience periods when our concerns about one particular aspect of our lives are so pronounced that it's extremely tough to deal effectively with other aspects of our lives. I know a writer, for instance, who becomes so absentminded when he is in the final phases of a writing project that he sometimes forgets where he parks his car. And while the stereotype of the absentminded professor has probably been exaggerated, the world of science is filled with men and women who are capable of solving some of the most highly complex mathematical problems but have trouble remembering to bring home a quart of milk from the grocery.

Preoccupation and absentmindedness are one thing; persistent, irrational behavior is something else again. To illustrate irrational behavior, let me tell you about one of the most extreme examples of target obsession I've ever encountered in my practice.

It involved an intelligent, educated young man named Roy. Roy was dating a girl and was worried about the possibility of her becoming pregnant. In targeting terms, we could say that this young man's target was to prevent pregnancy.

As targets go, there was nothing out of the ordinary about this particular target. Nor is it a target difficult to achieve these days, given the accessibility of birth-control devices. But for a number of different reasons, one of which had to do with the strain Roy was experiencing on a new job, Roy's preoccupation with his target eventually evolved into an obsession. It wasn't enough that he and his girl friend never had intercourse. Worse, he lost his ability to make sensible judgments. One night at midnight I received a call from him. His voice was trembling. He and his girl friend had been petting and he had ejaculated into his trousers. What he wanted to know (remember, Roy was a college graduate) was whether it was possible for sperm to penetrate several layers of clothing and enter the girl's vagina, thereby causing her to get pregnant. Once I assured him over the phone that pregnancy was impossible under the conditions he described, he was able to relax that night but the obsession remained with him.

This example is an extreme one, but it illustrates the pattern: an irrational line of behavior resulting from an *obsessive* involvement with a target. As in most cases of target obsessiveness, the target itself was reasonable enough, but the thinking and the actions of the person pursuing the target were definitely not. His intense concentration on his target had in fact become a quite unhealthy obsession.

Recognizing Target Obsession in Your Own Life

It is the nature of target obsession that the people victimized by it are generally not aware of the condition. The irrational

behavior that symptomizes target obsession doesn't develop
overnight; it has a way of creeping up on you gradually, in
much the same way that alcoholism or drug addiction develops.

I recall one of my instructors in medical school who started
a coin collection. At first, he spent a couple of minutes during
our class sessions telling us about his new hobby, which was a
nice change of pace for us. By the time the term was nearly
over, our entire session was being taken up by our instructor's
musings about his coins. He'd become so involved with the
coins that he was unable to see the way in which he was ne-
glecting his other responsibilities.

Perhaps you know similar people—people who are joggers,
tennis players, or golfers, who can talk about nothing *but* the
sport they play, people whose interest in their sport disrupts
other aspects of their lives. But remember the measuring
stick we are using: It is not the *interest* but the *effect*. You
can love to jog, to play tennis, to play golf and, for that matter, to collect coins, but when your interest becomes so over-
whelming that nothing else in your life matters, you have
crossed the line between involvement and target obsession.
You are no longer target-oriented, but target-obsessed. In the
end, you will usually suffer for it.

In severe cases a target obsession can actually be an escape
mechanism that enables you to move your focus away from
areas of conflict and anxiety in your personality. The executive who lives and dies for his job is often (though not always)
a person who is plagued with self-doubts, riddled with tension and insecurity. Mothers who become obsessively involved with their children are often compensating for something missing in their lives.

None of which makes the problem of identifying and dealing with target obsession any easier. Target-obsessive behavior, as I've said, doesn't develop overnight, nor can it be
eliminated overnight. The only really effective way to deal

with the problem is to recognize its symptoms early enough, *before* the involvement you have with a target begins approaching obsessive proportions.

Common Forms of Target Obsession

Although target obsession is a condition that can crop up in any area of your life, certain patterns characterize large numbers of people. Let's look into some of them.

THE LOVING PARENT

Most parents share similar targets when it comes to their children. We all want our children to grow up as healthy, happy individuals, able to make their way in the world. But the emotional components of parenting, crucial as they are to the psychological well-being of a child, can often sabotage our efforts to reach our target. For children not only need love, guidance, and attention, they need room to grow and develop their own personalities.

As with all cases of target blindness, the difference between a healthy involvement and a disruptive involvement is largely one of degree. Consider:

ON-TARGET INVOLVEMENT	TARGET OBSESSION
Enjoying the company of your child. Wanting to spend much of your free time with the child.	Enjoying the company of your child to the *exclusion* of *everything else*. Wanting to spend *all* your free time with the child.
Being alert to possible dangers that could affect your child's health and safety.	Being in a constant state of apprehension that something harmful is going to happen to your child.
Sharing with relatives and close friends your feelings and reactions about your child.	Talking about nothing else *but* your child to friends, relatives and acquaintances.
Wanting to develop a sense of companionship with your child, and being able to pursue some common interests.	Insisting on being your child's best friend and confidant. Wanting to "re-live" your own youth with your child.

THE GO-GETTER

Wanting to get ahead in your career is one of the most common and healthiest targets you can have in your life. But an overly intense involvement with this target can not only disrupt your life, it can actually hold you back. Contrary to what popular fiction might lead you to believe, you don't have to be singlemindedly ruthless to move up the corporate ladder. The men who get ahead, by and large, know how to broaden their lives, and don't isolate themselves in their work. You need a certain amount of detachment from questions of success or failure to be effective.

Several studies on top-ranking corporate executives reinforce the point. A study of corporate presidents by the management consultant firm Heidrick and Struggles, for instance, has shown that while for most of these men their business *is* their chief interest, they still find time for community service, for family involvement, and for an active leisure life.

ON-TARGET INVOLVEMENT	TARGET OBSESSION
A keen interest in your job, your company, and your co-workers.	An interest in virtually nothing but your job, your company, and your co-workers.
A willingness to work extra hours when the situation demands.	A pattern of always working extra hours, even when the work can be handled by others.
The ability to delegate some responsibilities to subordinates	A fear that if you delegate responsibility to subordinates the job will not get done well or will be done so well the subordinate may be given credit you yourself want.

THE PERFECTIONIST

Perfectionism is one of the more subtle forms of target obsession but one of the most self-defeating. One of the problems with this concept is that the idea of striving for perfection is generally looked upon as a positive characteristic. The person who strives for perfection, the perfectionist, whether an artist, a craftsman, a chef, or an executive, usually attracts our admiration. And why not? Who wouldn't admire a person who expects no less than the best out of himself?

But there is another side of perfectionism that isn't talked about so much—perfectionism for its own sake. Striving for excellence and the achievement of perfection is one thing. Being blinded by it is something else again. The realist strives for perfection even while realizing the target can never truly be reached, yet he keeps on with the attempt. Too often a target-obsessed "perfectionist" is really looking for an excuse to avoid reality. Never satisfied by less than the perfect, he is easily able to rationalize failure.

Perfectionism can be a source of enormous energy, but it can also be a crutch, as it was for Greta, a young woman who wanted to write poetry but never got around to sending any of her poems to the various poetry magazines. She was too busy *perfecting* them.

The real danger of perfectionism as a way of looking at targets is that it gives you an easy excuse for failure. A famous tennis player, known for his classic strokes, once admitted that by trying to hit every shot "perfectly," he really made it easier for himself to accept defeat. "I could always tell myself," he said, "that I lost because I was trying to hit the ball *right*. Deep down I knew that I was giving myself a chance to lose."

Once more, let me emphasize the difficulty in separating target-oriented behavior inspired and motivated by a sense of perfectionism from target-oriented behavior completely dominated by perfectionism. Target-obsessed perfectionists are people who win battles but lose wars, people who never reach their targets because the closer they get to their targets, the further away they move them.

Combating Target Obsession

Target obsession is by no means an easy condition to cope with. Practically speaking, there are three ways to minimize the consequences of target obsession in your own life.

1. Be willing to accept the possibility that target blindness exists in your own behavior occasionally.
2. Get into the practice of taking the "long view" as well as the "short view."
3. Force yourself, where practical, to remove yourself temporarily from a situation where the possibility of target blindness may exist.

ACCEPTING THE POSSIBILITY OF
TARGET OBSESSION

What would you do if a good friend told you that you show much more love and concern toward your son than toward your daughter? Chances are you'd probably say, "Nonsense, I treat both of them the same."

But what if your friend were right? What if you did indeed favor one child over another but were so close to the situation you could not see it?

The willingness to accept the possibility of your own target obsessions is probably your chief line of defense against them. There's nothing morally wrong with having blind spots. Nearly everybody has them at one time or another. The president of a multinational corporation is just as susceptible to a target obsession as the man who shines his shoes each day.

So the rule is simple: Stay on the alert. Entertain the possibility that you may be a victim occasionally. If you catch even a suggestion that you might be losing your sense of proportion because of the intense glare of a target you're too focused on, accept the possibility of target obsession and do your own personal investigation.

STEPPING BACK TO AVOID TARGET BLINDNESS

Get too close to a target and you lose sight of it. You're suffering, in other words, from target blindness. That's why, regardless of what target you pursue, every now and then step back from it to get a larger picture of it. Artists do this all the time, working at the canvas for several minutes, then stepping back to get a feeling for how the painting looks from a short distance. The short distance provides a perspective that is impossible to achieve when you're right on top of a painting.

Get into the habit of "stepping away" every now and then

Target blindness is being too close to a problem—so
close that the target can hardly be identified. It is, simply,
not being able to see the forest for the trees.

from situations you feel particularly close to. It's not difficult to do. Wait for a quiet time. Now start thinking about the targets you're pursuing. Most people are logical enough so that when they are not caught up in the immediate emotion of a situation, they can usually decide for themselves what is sensible and what is not sensible behavior.

Florence, the mother of the fifteen-year-old daughter with the messy room, was able to develop the necessary perspective to combat her target obsession by drawing up a list of her daughter's "good" qualities and "bad" qualities. The fact that the list of "good" qualities was many times longer than the list of "bad" qualities was itself enough to give this woman a clearer focus on her situation.

In a later chapter we'll be talking about a concept I call target inventory, in which I'll explain how you can systematically maintain a perspective on the various targets in your life. For now it's enough to say that if every once in a while you do nothing more than analyze a situation in your life by sitting down and writing on a piece of paper the elements of the situation that are troubling you, you will be amazed at how things will fall into place. Granted, there are certain situations where the behavioral dynamics are so complex that you can't figure them out on your own. But most of the time, with a little distance and a little clear thinking, you should be able to recognize your blind spots and take the appropriate action.

GETTING AWAY FROM IT

Absence not only makes the heart grow fonder, it helps the mind think more clearly. Regardless of how deeply you are committed and how strongly you feel about a target, make it a point to put that target out of sight for a short period of time. Doing this will accomplish two things: 1. It will help prevent, or at least lessen, the possibility of your involvement burgeoning into an obsession; and 2. It will frequently give you new insights into that target.

Putting a target out of sight is possible in all but a handful of cases. Spending an occasional weekend in which you don't give one iota of thought to your job is not going to jeopardize your chances for promotion. If anything, your job performance will be better. You'll arrive at work on Monday morning with a fresher perspective.

Athletes talk about the danger of overtraining, of being overprepared. The danger of overdoing doesn't apply only to athletes. As I stressed over and over in the chapter on scheduling, it isn't so much the *time* you spend on a particular target that will determine whether or not you reach that target, it is *how* you use that time. It's just as easy to miss a target by trying *too* hard than it is to miss by not trying hard enough. Finding the balance that works for you is, of course, one of the keys to targeting. But to find that balance, you need perspective. And nothing helps develop perspective more than setting an occasional distance between you and the targets that mean the most to you.

TARGET PRACTICE 8

Testing Your Susceptibility to Target Obsession

The toughest part of being target obsessed is recognizing it in yourself. But if you're aware of the fact that you have a tendency toward this often self-destructive variation of targeting, you can frequently take steps to develop the necessary perspective. The following brief test is designed to give you an idea of your susceptibility to target obsession. Choose the answer that best describes you:

1. I make decisions I later regret.
    a. Frequently
    b. Sometimes
    c. Hardly ever

2. Being "right" is terribly important to me.
    a. Frequently
    b. Sometimes
    c. Hardly ever

3. Once I make up my mind to do something, I'm determined to follow it through to the end.
    a. Frequently
    b. Sometimes
    c. Hardly ever

4. It's hard for me to enjoy myself if I know I've left a job undone.
    a. Frequently
    b. Sometimes
    c. Hardly ever

5. It bothers me to lose an argument.
    a. Frequently
    b. Sometimes
    c. Hardly ever

6. It's hard for me to admit that I'm wrong.
    a. Frequently
    b. Sometimes
    c. Hardly ever

7. I believe it's important to "stick to your guns."
    a. Frequently
    b. Sometimes
    c. Hardly ever

8. Once I get started on something, my approach is to barrel through and finish it.
    a. Frequently
    b. Sometimes
    c. Hardly ever

9. It's easy for me to remove myself from a situation and view it objectively.
    a. Hardly ever
    b. Sometimes
    c. Frequently.

How to score:

Give yourself 3 points for every (a) answer; 2 points for every (b) answer; and 1 point for every (c) answer. If your total was under 12, you probably don't have a tendency toward target blindness. A score of between 13 and 18 indicates a slight tendency toward it. And anything over 18 puts you in the high-risk category. Maybe you should reread Chapter 8.

CHAPTER 9

Overcoming Obstacles
to Targeting

Now that you've read this far, you should be well on your way to an understanding of the targeting process. It may be that you've begun to use some of the techniques we've been talking about. But it's also possible that, in trying to incorporate some of these techniques into your life, you've run into some obstacles—obstacles that have kept you from achieving the targets you have established for yourself, in spite of all your efforts.

What kind of obstacles am I talking about?

Well, for one thing, are you one of those people with a large library filled with books you've started but never finished? (Don't worry, you are not alone; there are plenty of us!)

Or are you the sort of person who signs up for two or three adult-education courses in the fall but by Christmas has drifted away, lost interest, and is no longer going to class? Is your brain bursting with ideas and projects—for new businesses, for trips, for strategies for living or working—but do you find these targets are never realized, and the ideas, alas, never translated into reality? In other words, are you one of those persons who has no trouble establishing targets, but a lot of trouble following through on them?

On the other hand, you may be a person who has no problem getting things done once you get started, but a lot of trouble getting started. I know many such people—gifted, intelligent, competent people—who are the victims of persistent inertia, who are stalled long before they even get their engines running.

And even if you don't happen to fall into either of these categories, there's a better-than-even chance you often run into certain obstacles that can plague even the most target-minded person. If you are like most people, in fact, you may frequently be victimized by those inexplicable obstacles that interfere with successful targeting, obstacles that are often referred to as "mental blocks."

This chapter is about those very mental blocks, those specific problem areas which can inhibit the targeting process. There *are* means to cope with those obstacles, and this chapter will show you some tested ways to combat them. Read on.

Why Goals Are Necessary

Establishing a target is an act of affirmation. Any time you set up a target, the assumption you make is that you have a good chance of reaching your target. Inherent in that action is confidence in your ability to achieve your goal.

Setting a target also implies a belief in the value of that target or goal.

By the very act of establishing a target, therefore, you have expressed a belief in yourself, an attitude of optimism about life and your chances for success.

On the other hand, not being able (or not wanting) to set targets for oneself is an expression of a negative attitude. A curious characteristic about people who have trouble setting targets for themselves is the way they often rationalize this difficulty. They act as if the absence of targets in their lives were a virtue and not a liability. "I just want to take things as they come," a troubled nineteen-year-old college student used to say to me over and over again when he came regularly to see me two years ago. "I want to live day to day, and enjoy every moment for what it is." In a current phrase, he thought he wanted to "go with the flow."

These are poetic sentiments, I grant you, but this was the same young man who, while hitching a ride one afternoon from Connecticut to New York, discovered from the first driver who stopped to pick him up that he was on the wrong side of the highway. He was, in fact, on his way to Boston. "That's okay," the young man said, "I'll go to Boston instead."

There may be something refreshing in this attitude on occasion, but it is hardly a practical or very reasonable approach to most of life's needs. And buried beneath its seeming casualness is, in reality, a negative approach to just about everything. Life is not so simple that we can all take this *laissez-faire,* take-it-as-it-comes approach.

I question whether it is really possible to derive any satisfaction or fulfillment unless there is at least some direction or focus in your life. To make no choices, to set up no goals, is to deprive life of its interest and meaning. The hippies and "flower children" of the 1960s had some valid arguments when they rebelled against the materialistic values of American society, but their failure to establish a true set of *alternate* values led to the collapse of their way of life. Humans are problem-solving animals. We need objectives. We need focus and direction. Most of all, we need the sense of accomplishment that comes from achieving what we set out to do. Without this sense of accomplishment, a true sense of self and of self-esteem is virtually impossible to develop.

What's Holding You Back?

Any number of influences beyond your control can determine whether or not you reach your targets, but nothing can prevent you from establishing the target in the first place—nothing, that is, but yourself. Sounds simple but, of course, it's not. We human beings are complicated pieces of work and much goes into determining how and why we act as we do. Many things prevent us from taking the crucial first step in the targeting process. For some it is a fear of failure and disappointment. Such people have the idea that the more you want something, the more it will hurt if you don't get it. Such people are afraid to risk failure and the supposed hurt it can bring.

Another common fear that interferes with targeting, odd as it may sound, is the fear not of failure, but of *success.* This failure seems to stem from an unrecognized, subconscious feeling that somehow one is not really worthy of the success that on a conscious level one is striving for. Many women in American society have this problem, a consequence of their perceived sense of woman's worth in a society dominated preponderantly by male values, goals, and attitudes. For others, the problem can be a lack of basic self-confidence. The chief symptom of such a lack of belief in oneself is the tendency to exaggerate the difficulty of a target, which discourages such people from even establishing the target.

Finally, there are those people who approach life with a totally fatalistic view. Such people will tell you that no matter what you do, things will turn out the way fate intends them to turn out. Personal effort, they feel, is of little use in a world in which all things are predetermined.

Fear of disappointment, fear of success, a lack of self-confidence, an overly fatalistic view of life—any one of these factors is usually enough to short-circuit the targeting process even before the process has a chance to begin. Any one of these factors can be enough to prevent you from taking the one step that, more than any other, will determine whether or not you're going to solve a problem or accomplish a task. If you are restrained from setting up your own targets by any one of these inhibiting factors, there is no way you will be able to envision that problem or task as a target around which you can construct a target-oriented strategy. But there are various (and proven) ways to counter such difficulties.

Talking Yourself into It

If it is true (and it usually is) that the only person preventing you from establishing targets is yourself, it follows that the only person who can get you out of this dilemma is *you*. Not until you can transcend your fear of failure or success, not until you can develop a certain amount of self-confidence, and not until you can modify your paralyzing fatalism will you be able to break through the barrier that keeps you from taking a more active, more target-oriented approach to your life. The agonizing truth here is that the best ammunition needed to fight these obstacles is itself on the other side of that barrier. This ammunition is the sense of accomplishment that is gained from the experience of reaching a target you've set for yourself.

It is never purely accidental that we fear failure or success, that we lack self-confidence, or that we refuse to believe that we ourselves can be the architects of our destiny rather than the victims of it. These "built-in" attitudes are reactions to past experience. Events in our lives lead us to assume a point of view that reflects our past history. Much of this experience occurs in our lives long before we can be fully aware of it— when we are children. People with a history of failure are not very likely to have much self-confidence. People who have been hurt and disappointed frequently are not likely to place themselves in situations where additional hurt and disappointment is likely.

These patterns, these learned modes of thought and behavior need not become a fixed part of your life. Not at all! You can control your life and you can do something about old patterns. For if the way you think today is a reflection of what happened to you yesterday and the day before, it is certainly reasonable to suggest that if you take certain steps today—

difficult as those steps may be—you can produce a different point of view tomorrow, a point of view that will make it easier for you to take other, similar steps.

There is only one way to deal effectively with obstacles that may now be preventing you from establishing targets for yourself. First of all, you must recognize and acknowledge the source of the problem. And the source of the problem, for whatever reasons, is you yourself. Once you recognize this, you'll be ready to deal with the problem.

It may not be easy. I'm not suggesting that it is. There are undoubtedly some real, well-founded reasons that you think the way you do. But if you experience difficulty in doing what you want to do, there are ways and means to change that situation. And in most cases you should be able to reverse the patterns you want to reverse on your own. Here is an exercise that may help. To do this exercise, you need only a large piece of paper and a pen or pencil.

An Exercise in Target Construction

Start by thinking up a target that you may have thought about in the past but have never acted upon. Maybe it involves learning how to play an instrument, or setting up a physical-fitness program, losing weight, or learning a new language. If you have trouble thinking of a target in this category, try to isolate an area of your life currently giving you some trouble—a relationship you may have, or something involving your job. Set up the solving of that problem as a target.

Now that you have determined a potential target, take a large piece of paper, and write the problem across the top of the page. Divide the rest of the sheet into three columns. Now, head the first column "Why I want to reach this target." Head the second column "Obstacles," and head the third column "Why this is not a real obstacle."

At this point concentrate on the first column. Think hard and list all the reasons you can for why you want to reach this target. Be as specific as you can. Don't even think about possible obstacles at this point.

It's crucial that you *not*—repeat, *not*—deal with the Obstacle column before you finish the first column. Too many people tend to do this in the normal course of their lives. What they do is concentrate on talking themselves out of a potential target before they've even had a chance to ponder the potential benefits and desirable advantages of their targets.

Now, in the second column, list the possible obstacles to your target. Stick to the subject here, too. Don't worry about why an obstacle isn't really an obstacle yet. Simply list as many reasons as you can think of as to why you may not be able to reach the target you want to set for yourself.

Surprisingly enough, if you're like most people you may not have to go any further with this exercise. It will become immediately apparent to you that there are really no major obstacles, no real reasons why you shouldn't pursue the target you want. It may be easy and all too human, for instance, to say "I can't do that," but it's very much something else to come up with specific reasons to back up this defeatist claim. Writing reasons down in a column forces you to focus on specifics. Often such an exercise proves that there really aren't specific reasons for not doing something—none, at any rate, of any real substance. Nevertheless, let's assume for the moment that you have indeed isolated real obstacles. This means that you should now proceed to the next phase of the exercise—examining those obstacles carefully, exploring why in fact they may not be real obstacles.

Oh yes, by posing the question the way we've posed it, I realize we've stacked the deck against the obstacle. That is precisely the purpose of this exercise! The point here is to motivate you to counteract the negative impluses that so far have been preventing you from establishing targets.

Let me give you a hint for the best way to attack the third phase of this exercise. Pretend for the moment that you're someone else—someone whose job it is to talk you into this particular target, a sort of "positive advocate" for targeting. As the "positive advocate," start with the premise that all the obstacles *can* be overcome. Assume that the problem is simply a matter of coming up with the right approach. Most important of all, be sure to deal with only one obstacle at a time. If you find you can't come up with a reason why a particular obstacle isn't an obstacle, go on to the next obstacle.

It's entirely possible that when you have finished this exercise, you will have many more items written in the second column than in the third column. This is to say, you won't be able to come up with reasons to discount the obstacles lying between you and your potential target. On the other hand, it's just as possible that once you begin to scrutinize each obstacle carefully, one at a time, you will realize that none of the obstacles you've been concerned with is insurmountable. And what you'll come to realize is that it isn't so much the obstacles themselves that have been keeping you from establishing targets, but rather the way in which you've been imagining these obstacles, the manner in which you have perceived them. In other words, you have been basing your response to a situation not on what actually is, but on what you *think* is.

For an example of how this kind of exercise might look after you've finished each step, see the chart on page 134.

TARGET: Learning How to Play Guitar

WHY I WANT TO REACH THIS TARGET	OBSTACLE	WHY THIS IS NOT A REAL OBSTACLE
1. To have a new interest that will bring me pleasure.	1. I'm not very musical.	1. It doesn't necessarily take great musical skill to enjoy the guitar.
2. I'll be fulfilling a dream I've always wanted to fulfill.	2. Guitars and guitar lessons are expensive.	2. Guitars are frequently on sale; there are also inexpensive lessons available at the Y and other places.
3. I'll be developing an interest that will help me meet people.	3. I don't have the time to devote to lessons and practice.	3. I'll spend less time watching television.
4. If I learn how to play the guitar, I won't be bored anymore on evenings when I don't go out.	4. I've never stuck to any lessons in the past; why should this time be any different?	4. The reason I'll stick to lessons this time is that I will make up my mind to do so. (I'll pretend to be determined.)

This exercise is not intended to help you reach your target. Its purpose is to get you to a stage where you are willing to establish a true target for yourself. Will the exercise work for everybody in every situation? No. But if you find it difficult to set targets for yourself, or follow through on them, going through such an exercise could very well reverse the pattern. And once you've had success in reversing a pattern, you should find it easier to generate the kind of target-oriented behavior that feeds upon itself and produces the confidence and self-trust you may now be lacking.

How to Dig In

On the face of it, the easiest part of any target-oriented task should be getting started. Early in a project you don't have to deal with deadline pressure, so you can be selective about which aspect of the target you address yourself to first. Generally, too, you bring to a new undertaking a fresh perspective that you don't always maintain midway through the process or near the end.

At the start you tend to have more energy. You're not as familiar with the target or its attached problems. You're not apt to be bored by it. And yet for some people, getting started, digging in, or getting into the right groove is the single most difficult part of any task. It is a common enough failing, but the problem seems particularly prevalent among creative people. Some writers I know talk as if they'd rather be flogged than experience the agony and frustration they feel whenever they are forced to sit down in front of that first piece of blank paper and commit to type the first words of an article, story, or essay.

One writer describes this agony as his "sharpening pencils syndrome." "I start out in the morning," he says, "by sharpening all the pencils I can get my hands on, even though I never use more than two or three pencils a day. I'll even go looking for pencils when I can't find any more on my desk. Once my pencils are sharpened, I can usually find a few books out of place on my shelves, and so I take a few minutes to put them back where they belong. By this time my coffee needs to be heated up and so I have an excuse to go into the kitchen. Finally, after an hour or two, I've run out of excuses and I manage to sit myself down in front of the typewriter."

Not that this phenomenon is found exclusively among writers. Executives I know report much the same thing in corporate offices each week. "It's like a zoo," reports one vice-president of a food company. "Everybody shuffling back and forth from office to office, visiting, getting coffee, delaying until the last possible moment the actual moment they start work."

In moderation, what I'm describing is a common enough and harmless enough practice—nothing to be concerned about. It's the rare person, after all, who can jump straight into the thick of a task. Most tasks require an "easing in" of sorts. Athletes go through a warm-up routine before the actual competition begins. Singers have to warm up their voices. Dancer have to limber up. It's all part of getting the body primed, getting the blood flowing. The same principle seems to hold true for mental activity as well.

There's also an energy principle at work here. To paraphrase Newton, it takes more energy to generate movement from an inert state than it does to accelerate movement once you're already in motion. The principle holds true for electrical appliances, for automobiles, etc., and it appears to hold true for people as well. Getting started on a task—and, in particular, getting started in the right direction—obliges us to expend a good deal more effort than we have to expend once we've already established some momentum.

Another factor at work in the starting phase is *feedback.* You are never further away from your target than you are at the very start of a task or project. For many people the distance to the target in itself is a problem. Once we're well launched into a task, we can detect tangible signs of progress. This is positive feedback, and this feedback usually acts to spur us onward, encourage us to further effort. But when there are no tangible signs of progress (which, of course, is always the case in the beginning of a project), we have either to generate our own positive feedback or else get along without it—a difficult challenge for many.

Practically speaking, there is no way you can completely eliminate these characteristics of the getting-started process. The problem of inertia and the lack of positive feedback are givens. You can't rewrite the basic laws of physics. You can't change basic motivational and feedback patterns. But what you *can* do is employ a few techniques that take into consideration some of the difficulties inherent in getting started on the right track—techniques that recognize the special conditions that prevail in the beginning stages of a targeted task.

Not all of the techniques I will suggest here may work for you—much about your choice has to do with your job, your work habits, your personality, and your temperament. Still, by familiarizing yourself with the various techniques, and by experimenting with a few of them, I feel sure you will be able to find one or two that will alleviate, if not entirely eliminate, the problem of getting on track each day.

Anticipatory Targeting

A music arranger I knew discovered that if he left an arrangement in midphrase the day before when he stopped working, it was easier for him to start on the arrangement the next day. I have heard of writers who break off their writing in midsentence the same way. This practice of "starting where I left off" avoids one of the more persistent problems that arise when you're first beginning in the morning. It's a means of insuring an immediate start when next you pick up the work,

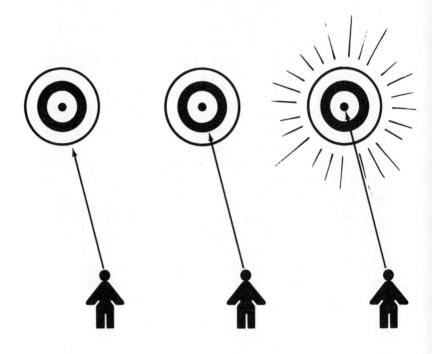

Anticipatory targeting is a targeting procedure for people who have trouble getting started. The answer is "positive grooving"—getting a running start by doing part of a job. Success at one stage creates motivation for going on.

because it provides you with a continuing thought line to begin with again.

There is no reason why the same practice can't work for people in other lines of work. Indeed, it does work well for many people. There are variations, too, on the habit of leaving something in midstream so as to ease right back into it when you resume work: "What I do the last twenty minutes or so at work the afternoon before determines how easy it is for me to start being productive the next morning," explains Hal P., a marketing executive who is one of the most productive people I know. He adds, "I don't only write out a list of what I want to do the next day. I try to assemble as many of the things I'll need to get started, so that when I come in the next morning, it's all set. I'm geared for action."

The logic is sound. Tired though you may be at the end of a workday, your mind is still in a more focused groove than it will be first thing in the morning. More's the reason, then, to save at least ten minutes of every workday for setting yourself up for the following day. For myself, I have discovered that it is more difficult for me to organize my thoughts and get into a productive work groove on days when my desk is cluttered than on days when it is in order. I make it a practice, as much as I can, to spend a few minutes in the late afternoon putting my desk in order.

You can apply the same principle to household chores. Remember the cellar so badly in need of clearing out? You've resolved to clean it up, but for two weekends, you've managed to fritter away the morning you've set aside to do the job. Try to change your pattern. This weekend, for a change, try getting everything you need—buckets, rags, cleaning liquids, even the clothes you are going to wear—ready the night before.

Are you a jogger who sometimes finds it difficult to get started on your workout each morning (as many joggers do)? Try to have everything you need—your running shoes, warm-up suit, etc.—set out right by your bed, so you don't have to go searching around for them as soon as you wake up the next morning. Remember, if you give yourself an excuse for not starting (and what better excuse can you give yourself than not being able to find your sneakers?), you're all too likely to use that excuse to put off—and maybe even postpone—the desired activity. *Deprive yourself of easy excuses* and you'll go a long way to limiting the delaying tactics that may be keeping you from getting the most out of your life.

GETTING DISPLACEMENT TO WORK FOR YOU

There is a phenomenon in psychology known as "displacement" in which one experience has a "carry-over" effect on another experience, even though the experiences are different. When this happens, feelings aroused or reactions caused by one experience may be repressed for the moment, only to surface quite unexpectedly and inappropriately in another situation.

Displacement can work for you or against you. It works against you when a tough day at work puts you in such a sour mood that you start to quarrel with everyone in your family as soon as you get home. But let's examine here how the same phenomenon can work *for* you, especially when it comes to getting you off on the right track in target-oriented tasks.

The idea is to transfer a positive attitude from one situation over to another one—the difficult one. If you have a difficult task ahead of you, purposefully precede that task with an activity you know will leave you with a feeling of accomplishment. The activity doesn't necessarily have to be related to the task at hand. One of the unexpected benefits of jogging early in the morning, for instance, is that it gets your day off on a strongly positive note. You've accomplished something. You've reached a target. You've generated positive momentum. You feel pleased with yourself, and your self-confidence enjoys the boost.

Jogging is hardly the only way to use displacement to good advantage. Another way is to juggle the order of interim targets related to a task or to a job. If you're a businessman who finds it hard to settle into a productive groove each morning, why not deliberately start your day with something you know you can handle easily? Start the day by writing a couple of letters or by putting the finishing touches on jobs that are 95 percent complete. Remember the techniques discussed in the chapter on scheduling. You may not be able to control what you have to do on a given day, but you can control *when* you do it. Arrange your schedule so that an hour or so after you've begun work, you will have something positive to show for your efforts. This small amount of arranged positive feedback can often generate the momentum you need to launch you into the more difficult tasks. It's a warm-up.

Another variation of the same technique involves the setting out of easily accomplished interim targets. Does the mere thought of cleaning out your cluttered attic fill you with exhaustion? Don't think about the whole attic. Look at one corner and set an interim target for yourself involving that corner alone. Have you run into problems organizing yourself for a large dinner you have to get ready for company? Pick out one small part of the meal and complete it. A lawyer I know uses this technique of setting up easily accomplished interim targets. He *deliberately* leaves his desk cluttered the night before. "It usually takes me about 15 minutes to get everything straightened out each morning," he explains. "And when I've finished, I feel as if I've already done something important and the feeling stays with me throughout the morning."

THE "TOE FIRST" PRINCIPLE

There are essentially two ways you can get yourself started on a task. One method is like taking a running jump into a swimming pool. The other is to ease slowly into the pool little by little, letting the body get accustomed to the water temperature. Some of us are "jumpers," and some of us are "toe firsters." It helps to know what sort of person you are when the time comes to get started on a task.

Carried to the extreme, probably neither one of these approaches is advisable. The "jump first, think later" approach is a sure-fire way of getting the juices flowing in a hurry, but it can also land you on tracks leading to blind alleys. On the other hand, a too cautious "toe first" approach can cause you to waste a lot of time.

Generally speaking, people with a strong measure of confidence and energy, people prepared for the possibility of making a couple of false starts, who are comfortable with the idea of "thinking on their feet" tend to do better with a "jump first" approach to tasks. "Let's quit talking about the script and start acting," Laurence Olivier is quoted as having said on many occasions. "We'll learn as we do." But if you don't fall into this category, don't feel compelled to take this approach. Experiment. Make up your mind one morning on your way to work that you're simply going to plunge right into whatever tasks lie before you at the office. See how you do with that approach. Try it for a couple of days and if you find yourself getting bogged down, then try something different until you find the rhythm that best suits your personality. There is nothing wrong with a "toe first" approach—just as long as it doesn't take you *too* long to get into the water.

Mental Blocks and How to Overcome Them

No matter who you are or what you do, no matter how adept you are at targeting, you are still likely from time to time to run into the phenomenon commonly known as a "mental block."

Being mentally blocked means, simply, getting stuck or being bogged down in a task for no apparent reason. As the term implies, the problem begins with the mind but its effects extend to physical activities, too. It can happen when you're trying to figure out a problem, or when you're writing a report. Everyone has heard of "writer's block," when a writer can't seem to get through a particular writing assignment. But the same thing can also happen when you're at a dance lesson or trying to learn a new chord on the guitar. Suddenly, you run into an invisible wall. You know what you want to do—you have a target—and there doesn't seem to be any reason why you *can't* do what you want. You have the ability and the means at hand. Still, no matter how hard you try you can't make any progress. Like a car mired in a mud bank, your wheels spin and spin but you stand still.

Many theories have tried to explain why and even how mental blocks occur. Sometimes they occur because of a drop in energy level—a drop you may not be aware of. You get mentally fatigued. If there is some doubt in your own mind about what you're doing, some conflict about your task, that could be another reason.

At other times mental blocks occur because of an overload of stimuli. Too much happens at one time for your brain to process all the information efficiently. Imagine a superhighway at rush hour on a morning when four lanes are suddenly forced to converge into one lane because of an accident. A similar jam-up occurs in the brain when we subject it to too much at one time.

What can you do in such moments when you get "blocked?" There are two different strategies that can work with mental blocks, but it's difficult to say which one will work best in which situation. One of them might be called the "battering ram" approach. You simply marshal all your energies, lower your head, and try to crash through the block. If the block is a mild one, the battering ram approach will work.

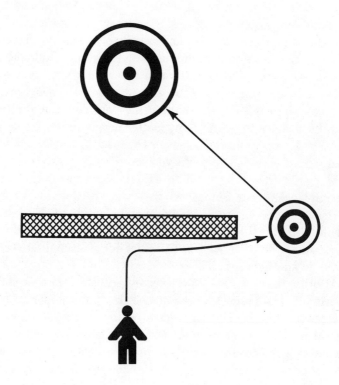

Positive sidetracking is a way to achieve a target that is obstructed. It involves nothing more complicated than going around the obstruction, usually by means of a subsidiary target or targets that show the way. The trick is to keep the main goal in mind.

Sometimes, in fact, this is the most practical and most sensible tactic to use.

But if the block is more significant, the battering ram approach will not only *not* work, it will worsen the situation. The more you try, the more impenetrable the invisible wall will appear, and the more frustrated you'll get trying to get through it.

When this happens, when a block doesn't yield to the application of more effort, here's something you can try: It's a technique I call *positive sidetracking.*

POSITIVE SIDETRACKING

Of all the tools you have at your disposal in your targeting arsenal, none is as potentially useful as the ability to use positive sidetracking—when the situation is ripe for it. Positive sidetracking means deliberately taking yourself off the track leading you toward your originally intended target and moving off in another direction altogether. True, by doing so you are taking yourself away from your intended target, just as if you were being victimized by a diversionary target, which we discussed earlier. But the difference between getting sidetracked by a diversionary target and positive sidetracking is that when you sidetrack you are conscious and aware of what you're doing and why you're doing it. You also control how long the sidetracking will continue. You don't lose sight of your target. You simply have made a decision that you feel is necessary for the best interests of ultimately achieving your target.

Positive sidetracking can vary from an activity of only two or three minutes to a strategy involving several weeks. The coffee break is a classic illustration of positive sidetracking. You take a break, getting off your original track for a different one, but you do not stray so far off the primary track that you can't easily resume your initial position. A broader illustration of positive sidetracking is the three-week break from tennis that the Swedish champion Bjorn Borg likes to take each year. "I go away for three weeks and try not to even think about tennis," Borg once said. "I don't bring my racquet, and I don't go near a court."

The need for positive sidetracking varies, of course, from person to person and from situation to situation, but it's safe to say that all of us need to try it from time to time. The problem is that some people are so intensely concerned about reaching a target that they fail to recognize when they are spinning their wheels without getting anywhere. Guilt and group pressure frequently inhibit us from making a positive sidetracking move when the situation warrants it. Too many of us take too literally the old adage, "When at first you don't succeed, try, try again." The adage is sensible enough on the surface but not very effective if what we really need is a little time to recharge our batteries. I'm not suggesting here that the minute you begin to sense any resistance to your efforts in a given task you immediately take a break or figure out something else to do. Just try to stay aware of the trap of "overtrying." Keep in mind the image of Br'er Fox pummeling the tar baby in the Uncle Remus story. The more he struggled, the more he became stuck. There is a stage in just about every difficult task where trying *harder* becomes counterproductive. You have to develop the sensitivity needed to tell when this stage is reached.

One of the most reliable barometers is your state of mind. Listen to yourself. Bjorn Borg knows it is time to do some positive sidetracking when he begins to lose his sense of self-control on the court. A journalist friend knows it's time when she starts making typing errors. Any change in your state of mind—getting angry, feeling frustrated, getting bored—can be a sign that it's time to pull back for a moment or two, time to regroup, time to recharge your mental batteries. In certain situations you may not have the luxury of a positive sidetracking alternative, but such situations are generally fairly rare. What is to stop you, for instance, from getting up from your desk when things are going poorly and doing five minutes of stretching or calisthenics? Nothing is stopping you— nothing, that is, but the false sense of urgency that makes it difficult for you to take your eyes away from the target for even a few minutes.

I said it earlier in the book, but I'll repeat it here: It isn't only the amount of time you spend on a task that will determine how successful you are in accomplishing that task. It's also the *quality* of effort expended. Two hours of effort, bisected with 15 minutes of positive sidetracking, can frequently do more in the way of real accomplishment than four hours of "solid work." Keep the principle of positive sidetracking in mind no matter what you're doing. And don't be afraid to use it when the time seems right.

TARGET PRACTICE 9

Getting Back on Track

It's a common enough occurrence. You're moving along well on a project or task when suddenly your concentration fails you and you run into what can best be described as a psychological stone wall. The reason could be fatigue or simply the fact that your mind is on something else— something more pressing. Whatever the reason, though, your main concern is to get back on track. Here are some specific suggestions, any one of which might work in any situation.

1. Take a Break

This is the most obvious—and the simplest—method of dealing with "mental blocks" and similar problem situations in which you find yourself bogged down in tasks for no apparent reason. Remember, though, the break you take is useless if you spend all of your time mulling over the problem you're facing. Try to get *away* from your work environment, even if it's only for ten or fifteen minutes. If you're at work, take a walk down the hall or go outside for a few minutes. Try to think about things that are far removed from your work but are not complicated enough on their own to further drain your mental energy. One advertising executive I know uses as a break distraction a long list of batting averages of major-league players that he looks over whenever his concentration on the job starts to fail him. Keep in mind, though, that the important characteristic of a work "break," regardless of how short or how long, is that it diverts your mind from the problem at hand.

2. Jump Ahead

Frequently in multiple-target situations it isn't necessary to follow a specific sequence of interim targets. So if you find yourself bogged down on one interim target, it's sometimes a good idea to set aside that target for awhile and work on a different aspect of the task. There comes a point, of course, when you run out of alternate targets to turn to in a targeting situation, but you probably have more flexibility in most situations than you think. And to get more and more bogged down in one task when there are several other tasks that are equally important is a foolish practice that rarely produces positive results.

3. Mentally Rehearse the Completion

Mental rehearsal or, as many people call it, visualization, is a technique that some people can use with excellent results while others find it virtually useless. The only way to find out how effectively the technique can work for you is to try it a few times in different situations. The trick behind mental rehearsal in the kinds of situations we've been dealing with is to create a mental picture of yourself completing the particular task or project that you happen to find yourself bogged down with. It's a self-psyching exercise whose purpose is to relax the mind and, in the process, rid your brain of whatever mental kinks are gumming up your mental faculties. I use mental rehearsal techniques often in my practice, especially with patients who have complicated personal problems. What we do is to create hypothetical situations in which the patient plays out different roles and takes note of his or her reactions. It doesn't work for everybody, but for some people, in some situations, it's a remarkably effective technique. Try it the next time you find yourself stuck on some problem. Sit back and for a moment or two picture yourself having already solved the problem and try to actually feel the relief and the pleasure that solving the problem can bring. The longer you can hold on to this feeling, the better the chances are that when you return to the problem, you'll return with renewed energy and a more focused sense of purpose.

4. Think Smaller

It's easy to be overwhelmed by the prospect of achieving certain difficult targets, and very often this feeling of being overwhelmed, in and of itself, can lead to the anxiety and the disorientation that produce inertia. The best way to attack the problem is to forget the overall target and concentrate instead on smaller, more easily reachable targets that, in the end, will help you reach the larger targets. As Dennis Ralston, the tennis coach, likes to tell the pros he works with, "Forget about the match, about the set, about the game. Just think about winning one point at a time."

CHAPTER 10

Taking Inventory

Taking inventory and keeping a running account of what items are in stock and what are out of stock are common practices in businesses. If you own a store, you need to know what's selling and what stock is lying around. You need to know whether the money you're investing in merchandise is or isn't working for you. Anybody in business who ignores basic inventory procedures is writing his or her own prescription for bankruptcy. I wonder, though, how many people apply this same principle to their own lives.

How about you? At this particular moment, for instance, are you really aware of where you stand in relation to the targets you've been setting for yourself? Do you know how far along you are in achieving those targets which are important to your life? Are you forever establishing targets and then losing sight of them in a few days, letting them gather dust in some remote section of your brain, unattended to and forgotten?

You may be thinking, "I'm too busy to sit down and take the time to take stock. I have plenty to keep myself occupied without adding something else to do!" Well, if you are not in the habit of keeping track of the targets you set for yourself, you are giving up one of the most important tools you have for living a productive life. Talk to people you know who are productive and happy. Chances are these people have a pretty clear idea of what they want out of life and how to go about getting it. Talk to people who are unhappy and lethargic, on the other hand, and there's a good chance you'll find people who are often confused about what they want to do with their lives and where they want to go with them.

Naturally, I am simplifying things. Simply being aware of your targets or where you stand in relation to them is no guarantee that you'll be a happier person or experience a greater sense of fulfillment in your life. But by and large it's safe to say that one of the main prerequisites for achieving a greater sense of fulfillment, for experiencing a larger sense of accomplishment in your life is having a sense of where you are.

And how can you obtain this special sense for your own life? One way is to establish for yourself what might best be described as a *target inventory.*

What Is a Target Inventory?

A target inventory is the sum total of whatever targets are present in your life at any given time. The number of targets in such an inventory will vary from person to person, as will the nature of these targets. Indeed, in your own life the number and nature of these targets may vary considerably from month to month and year to year. You may be going after targets at this very moment that you weren't even contemplating a month ago. You may be looking for a new job or working on a new hobby. Or channeling a lot of energy right now into some family difficulty that suddenly appeared unexpectedly overnight. Life is full of incident and accident, and as I've mentioned before in earlier chapters, it isn't always possible to control the selection of the targets we pursue. Because of life's unpredictability, problems present themselves and we have to address ourselves to them. Our values change as we grow older. Our priorities change.

If it is not always possible to control *what* targets you must go after, it is still possible to be aware of *where* you are in relation to the various ends you are pursuing. It's not the targets you've chosen or why you've chosen them that concerns me here; the point is to be aware of where you are in relation to your goals. This awareness alone can be enormously helpful in giving you a sense of yourself and of your life's meaning.

Gaining such an awareness involves nothing more complicated than keeping tabs on your target inventory. You need a system that will give you a general idea at all times of where you are in your life and where you want to go. This doesn't require you to be so target-obsessed that there is no room in your life for flexibility, change, or diversion. If you can keep a general picture in view of your overall situation, however, the decisions you make in your life will not be solely the result of pressures of the moment, but will be in keeping with much more fundamental decisions you've made about who you are and what you want to do with your life.

Keeping track of your target inventory isn't as simple a task as you might think. It isn't something most people do naturally. Indeed, one of the main reasons so many people get sidetracked from the targets they set for themselves is that they simply lose sight of what they're trying to get done. As Alvin Toffler pointed out years ago in his widely read book *Future Shock,* and as social scientists have been telling us for years, many of us are victimized by a phenomenon known as "overchoice." We have so many options, some of us, so many different life styles to choose from, so many different ways to raise our families, spend our leisure time, that simply choosing which way to go has become an exercise in stress. Even more difficult, as we've seen in the chapter on overcoming obstacles, is staying on one track long enough to follow through on the objectives we establish. I've known people who decide in September to take one or two courses in adult education, but who end up, in June, having taken four or five and completed none. Switching tracks is perhaps too easy in our society, and unless we keep track of the switching, it's easy to get lost. Keeping track of your target inventory is the chief means you have to keep from getting lost.

The Mechanics of Target Inventory

Now that we've looked briefly at what a target inventory is, and the difficulties that can interfere with it, let's look at precisely how you can go about drawing one up for the purposes of your own life.

Just as businesses set aside certain times of the year to go over their inventory, so should you periodically set aside time to get a fix on where you stand in relation to the targets in your life. How often you will need to take this inventory of your targets will depend, in large part, on your way of life. If your life is relatively stable and your outlook is positive and optimistic, you can get away with doing a target inventory as infrequently as two or three times a year. If, on the other hand, you're going through a period of transition, or if you are the sort of person who is constantly establishing new targets for yourself, it's probably good to make a target inventory more often, perhaps as much as once a month if practical. The average person, I think, should take at least one major target inventory every year, and one minor inventory once every three months. If you find you are experiencing a prolonged period of unhappiness or dissatisfaction, I would say a target inventory is usually called for.

GETTING STARTED

To set up a target inventory, you must first of all single out the various areas of your life that have the most bearing on your sense of well-being. Your personal list will more than likely include most, if not all, of the following life areas:

- Health
- Marriage
- Children
- Job or career
- Financial situation
- Housing
- Social relationships
- Leisure activities

These are the major areas that concern us all, but if you can think of some areas that are important to you that I haven't included here, add them. By now you know that my purpose is not to tell you what targets to set for yourself; I want to show you how to better organize your life around those targets you have decided will bring you the most satisfaction and fulfillment.

Once you've listed the various areas that most affect your sense of well-being, you're ready to take stock of just where you are in each of these areas. The way to do this is to ask yourself the question: *How satisfied am I with this particular area of my life?*

I suggest that you answer with one of the three possibilities (or maybe for you there are more): 1. Very satisfied; 2. Satisfied but there's room for improvement; or 3. Dissatisfied.

The point here is not to win a medal for the most times you can answer with Number One. This is not a contest. The point of this exercise is for you to discover what areas of your life are possible sources of both positive and negative feedback. It will give you a chance to isolate those areas where some scrutiny is called for. You will have to think carefully each time you ask the question, but at this point don't think about the *why* of your answers, just identify your general feeling about each particular area of your life.

Now you have a general picture of where you stand in your life. You know which areas bring you satisfaction at a given time. You know—or should know—which areas at the moment are detracting from your sense of satisfaction. If you describe yourself as a "generally happy and fulfilled" person, your list should be filled mainly with specific answers reflecting this happiness. If you describe yourself as "not especially happy," your list should indicate the areas from which the unhappiness originates. At this point you're ready to sit down and construct some targets.

Get out some more paper. Or, better still, buy yourself a notebook. Set aside at least a page for each of the "target" areas you plan to concentrate on for the next few months. Write the specific area at the top of the page and then write down the following statement: *"I would be more satisfied with this area of my life if . . ."* Beneath that sentence supply as many answers as you can think of. Don't worry about how "practical" the answers you list are or are not. You'll have time to look into the practicality of each answer a little later. In general, however, try to keep each answer within realistic, reasonable limits of feasibility.

Let's say, for instance, that the area you're examining is your job. Your answers to the question "I would be more satisfied with this area of my life if . . ." might be any or all of the following:

> (if) I didn't have to work as many hours.
> (if) I didn't have to travel as much.
> (if) I didn't have so much "busy work" to do.
> (if) I had more responsibility.
> (if) my boss didn't pick on me as much.
> (if) I had more to do.

If the area under consideration were your marriage, some of your answers might be:

> (if) we shared more common interests.
> (if) our sex life were more exciting.
> (if) my husband (or wife) wasn't so critical of me.
> (if) I had more time to do things alone.

Let's see what you've accomplished. You've succeeded in doing two things:

1. You've pinpointed the target areas in your life which are causing you some distress.
2. You've narrowed down, at least to a degree, the specific elements of these target areas which are causing the problem.

What do you do now? Your next step is to make targets of these specific problem elements. Just convert each answer you've given into the positive statement of a target. Here, again, start the process without exercising any judgment as to whether you can or can't achieve the target. What we're dealing with here are theoretical possibilities. For example, your list of possible job targets (converted from your answers) might look like this:

1. Work shorter hours.
2. Cut down on my traveling.
3. Eliminate some of the "busy work."
4. Get more responsibility.
5. Improve my relationship with my boss.
6. Build more variety into my job.

Now you've identified some targets—specific ones—within the overall, primary target of removing the elements of dissatisfaction you have been feeling in connection with your work. In each case, these targets (e.g., work shorter hours) can be broken down into interim targets. You probably can't attack each one simultaneously, so you'll have to consider priorities, target sequencing, and practicality. Perhaps now would be a good time to look back at the beginning chapters of this book to see how the techniques we've discussed can be used to help in your targeting actions.

Once you've reached this point, you're ready to put into practice some of the techniques we've been talking about throughout the book, like target construction and target sequencing. The only thing I can add to what we've already gone over is the importance of keeping tabs on your progress. Let's say you've established some specific targets designed to eliminate some of the busy work in your job—the work that's keeping you from handling larger responsibilities as well as you'd like to be handling them. A possible interim target in this area might be to "train my assistant to handle XYZ duties." Try and work this target into your schedule as soon as it's practical—within the next week, if possible.

Are you then finished with the targeting inventory aspects of this task? Not at all. At the end of this week or the beginning of the following week it's time once again to take inventory, to see whether or not you've addressed yourself to the target or targets you've set. If you've pointed yourself to the target and have followed through on it, you can cross that target off your list, but if you haven't, you need to ask yourself *why*. Were you diverted by other targets? Did you procrastinate? Were you simply too disorganized to pursue the targets? Did you fail to schedule properly? Could you have used a sweetening technique? Whatever the reason, try to get reorganized. Retarget the same task for the following week, and this time try to give it even *more* priority.

Taking Stock

If all goes well—and there is no guarantee, of course, that it will—the successful completion of your interim targets should help you achieve the primary targets you've set. Getting your assistant to take over some of your busy work, for instance, ought to be enough to eliminate or at least reduce this source of negative feedback in your life.

But don't take anything for granted. A month after you've taken your original inventory, it's time to take another look. Go back to your original list and *repeat the same process with all areas*—even those areas that were not causing you problems when you took your first inventory. It's possible, for instance, that in the month or so since your last inventory your life has undergone some changes. These changes, moreover, could very well be affecting any one of the key areas in your life—sometimes without your being aware of it. This is why it's so important to keep repeating the same inventory process. Try not to take anything for granted. Ask yourself the same basic questions in each area. Try, as much as possible, to keep a running account of what's working in your life and what isn't.

As curious as it may seem to you, the mere fact of being *aware* of the problem areas of your life tends to relieve the anxiety you can feel when you're unhappy and unfulfilled and don't know why. The awareness alone is not enough to solve the problem, but it can materially help you to work your way through it.

The process of taking target inventory is really not complicated. As we've seen, there are four phases:

1. Focusing on specific areas of your life (job, marriage, leisure, etc.) where you are less than satisfied about "where you are."
2. Narrowing down to the more specific aspects of these general areas.
3. Setting interim targets designed to improve the situation in each of these specific areas.
4. Periodical reviewing of your original target inventory to make sure you are, in fact, attending to the targets you've set for yourself.

How to Control Illusory Targets

It's possible that in taking target inventory from time to time you'll find that even though you've reached the targets you set for youself, your basic satisfaction level has remained the same or even worsened. How can this be? How is it possible to reach a target designed to improve your life, only to discover that the situation has not changed? The answer lies in a phenomenon I like to call *illusory targets*.

An illusory target is one that once reached yields feedback different from what was expected. It's the rare target, of course, whose feedback is exactly in line with expectations, but our concern here is with situations in which the gap between what we expect and what we actually receive is substantial. When we "succeed" but fail to experience the anticipated feeling of accomplishment or reward, the effect is almost always negative. Understandably so. And when this sequence of events happens frequently, it leads to confusion, disillusionment, and sometimes depression. What is going on, we might ask? Why do we confuse real with illusory targets? Where do they come from?

Why Illusory Targets Form

Illusory targets originate in two places. One has to do with society. The other has to do with the specific quirks in our personalities. Ours is a society with an economy fueled in large part by the creation of illusory needs. We all need food, shelter, and clothing, but in our consumer-oriented society a huge machine has as its end the job of making us buy and consume the products of our society. This machine, made up of the most sophisticated techniques of advertising, publicity, promotion, etc., never rests; it constantly exhorts us to pursue a great variety of targets, many of which are not even remotely related to our health and happiness.

It isn't enough, however, that the advertisements and commercials we see, hear, and read put such a disproportionate emphasis on, say, the wonders of owning powerful automobiles, buying the latest fashions, or drinking the peppiest colas. It is the implicit message being transmitted to us—the promise that by achieving these targets, we will realize benefits transcending the immediate rewards of the product itself.

It is the hidden promise of a tangible link between a woman's ability to take the dirt out of her husband's shirts and the happiness she should expect from marriage. Or that owning the latest high-powered machine—automobile, motorcycle, stereo—will make a man strong, sexy, smart, etc. I doubt that many people take these individual suggestions literally, but subliminally and cumulatively, the power of these promises has marked impact on the way many people view themselves in relation to others and to their position in the world.

Possibly the most troublesome area of illusory targets is in the world of sex. The overglorification of sex has permeated so much of what people read and see that it's only natural for people to question the quality of their own sexual lives. People begin to wonder if the sex they experience measures up to the models of whiz-bang sex they see used to sell various products. It's no longer enough to experience an orgasm—it has to "explode." It's no accident that impotence is on the rise in the U.S. It can't help but happen given the unrealistic models that many people are patterning their sex lives after.

As far as the second source of illusory targets—our own personalities—we have to recognize that the tendency to create illusory targets is a very natural one, but one which has to be held reasonably in check. If not, the targets you reach will invariably produce a letdown and not the sense of accomplishment you're looking for.

This doesn't mean you can't have fun anticipating things, or that you shouldn't occasionally fantasize. What's important, though, is that you be able to recognize the difference between an illusion and realistic expectation.

I know an author, for instance, who, at one stage of his career, was awaiting the sale of paperback rights to a book he had recently published. It was the sort of book that might have brought him anywhere from $10,000 to $200,000 in paperback rights. This particular man was fortunate. He had the ability to enjoy fantasizing about what his life would be like in the event the book sold for a big figure, but at the same time, he was aware of—but not upset by—the possibility that the price would be much less. As it turned out, the book *didn't* have a big sale, and while the author was understandably disappointed, he wasn't crushed or disillusioned.

Here we have a person who is able to balance his fantasy with reality, able to have fun with his fantasies but able to recognize, too, that you can't very well establish concrete targets on the basis of fantasy.

On occasion, an illusory target can be the result of a miscalculation or misjudgment, as in the case of Diane. Diane was forty-two years old, married, with children. After twenty years of raising her family and managing her household, she decided that she wanted to pursue a career outside the home. What prompted her decision more than anything else was a growing sense of dissatisfaction with the way her life was taking shape as her children grew older and more independent.

Diane set for herself a most reasonable target. She decided to get a degree in speech therapy. It took her two years, but she reached her target, inspired throughout by the conviction that once she was working in a job she liked, her life would have new meaning for her and would be filled with the satisfaction she'd been lacking.

But it didn't quite work out the way Diane had expected. Not long after she began working full time as a speech therapist, the feelings of dissatisfaction and depression that had originally led her to get her degree returned. At this point she came to see me. What I was able to discover after a few visits was that the true source of Diane's dissatisfaction had nothing to do with her career, but rather concerned her relationship with her husband.

It's useful here to review the exact nature of Diane's mistake. There was nothing wrong with the target Diane set up for herself, pursued, and realized. It was that the target was not in fact related to the real source of her problems. Therefore, the feedback from this target didn't make any meaningful difference in her basic predicament.

In Diane's case, at least, things worked out reasonably well. Once she was able to pinpoint the source of her unhappiness—her relationship with her husband—she was able to take steps to improve that area of her life. More importantly, though, she stopped expecting her job to compensate for the lack in the other areas of her life. Once she became aware of the true origins of her feelings, she began enjoying her work for its own sake. She doesn't have what could be called an "ideal" marriage, but because she's been able to sort things out for herself more clearly, she functions effectively and is quite pleased with the control she exerts over her life now.

Diane's example conveniently brings us back to the fundamental idea of this chapter: target inventory. I am convinced that most people have the ability to manage their lives effectively. The reason many people with this ability don't manage their lives more effectively is simply that they have failed to take the specific measures that produce the sense of mastery and awareness that underly the ability to manage a life in a productive and fulfilling manner. They fail to spend the time to take a true inventory of the goals in their lives.

Try it. Instead of simply keeping track in your mind of who you are and where you want to go, commit these ideas to paper. Set up your own inventory of targets. Do it frequently. Let the inventory be the instrument that keeps you on the track toward these targets you want to reach.

TARGET PRACTICE 10

Setting Up a Targeting "Score Card"

In addition to keeping an inventory on the various targets in your life, it's useful to keep tabs every now and then on the degree to which you're reaching targets on a daily basis. The following exercise, which should take no more than ten or fifteen minutes a day, is an excellent means of heightening target awareness and a good way to get some insight into just how target-oriented you really are.

You begin by taking about five or ten minutes at breakfast, or at your desk when you're just starting out at work in the morning, to simply write down the targets you hope to accomplish throughout the course of the day. Try to project realistically. That is, don't establish targets that you don't have a reasonable chance of reaching. But don't go too easy on yourself, either. Include both little targets—writing thank-you notes, picking up items you need at the hardware store, etc.—with larger targets involving your work or leisure. On a typical day you might have as many as twelve targets or as few as four. It doesn't matter. What does matter is that you spend some time each evening going over the list of targets you've set for yourself earlier in the day, putting a checkmark beside the targets you've reached, and an "x" beside the targets you haven't reached. You can consider it a successful week if you've had the same success for at least four of the five workdays.

If on the other hand, you're consistently failing to reach 70 percent of the targets you set, it means one of two things: 1. You're setting too many targets for yourself on a daily basis; or 2. You're not dealing as efficiently as you might with the targets you've established. To find out which is the case, try for a few days to cut down on the number of targets you set for yourself in the morning. Should you find yourself still falling well short, you can be reasonably certain that the fault lies less in the number or nature of the targets you're setting, and more in your method of pursuing these targets.

CHAPTER 11

Targeting in Action

Throughout this book I have tried to show you how, by the use of some fairly simple techniques, you can gain more control over the quality of your life, and how you can organize more effectively the way you employ your time and your own abilities. I have said over and over that if used intelligently, targeting can help you put your own skills and abilities to better and more effective use. Like any tool, it can be misused, but also like any tool, the more experience you have with it, the better you'll become at using it.

Developing such an awareness is a continuing learning process. Possibly some of the steps I've been recommending—setting up a schedule for yourself, keeping lists, keeping a diary of target inventory—may seem artificial or uncomfortably contrived to you at first. But with practice, these steps will come to seem natural. Remember the first time you tried to play the piano, or drive a car, or hit a tennis ball? In these situations, too, you probably felt self-conscious and uncomfortable. The learning of *any* new skill, whether physical or mental, is bound to produce feelings of awkwardness. So don't be discouraged.

One of the best features about targeting is that once you have incorporated aspects of it into the regular rhythm of your life, it becomes its own reinforcer. The feeling of accomplishment successful targeting can produce will increase your self-confidence. This increase, in turn, will make you more eager for new challenges. And new targets.

Something else, too. You may find that some of the targets you set for yourself will turn out (after you've reached them) to be targets you actually didn't want to reach in the first place. False targets, let's call them. Don't make the mistake of thinking that the time and effort that goes into the reaching of these "false" targets is necessarily wasted. Not a bit. For even if a target you set for yourself doesn't turn out to be exactly what you had in mind, the process of targeting and reaching that target can be a good learning experience, an experience whose benefits will make you that much more likely to reach other and more appropriate targets.

So trust your instincts and judgment. Except in those cases where your health or survival or the health and survival of other people are in jeopardy, don't dwell excessively on the possibility that a target you *think* you want to reach may not be a target you really are after. Many people waste a great deal of time worrying about making the "right" decision. I say make a choice in an open way, as freely as possible. Then concentrate on the targeting steps necessary—you can always change the target later.

Applied Targeting

Throughout most of this book, I've been talking about targeting in general terms. Now that you're familiar with some of the general concepts, let's take a look at some specific situations in life to see how some of these concepts can be utilized.

TARGETING ON THE JOB

The successful use of targeting techniques on the job begins with an understanding of the multiplicity of targets that prevail in most job situations. Basically, there are three targets to be addressed at work. The degree to which each target is important can vary enormously from job to job. The three are:

1. The mechanics of the job itself.
2. The "social" or "political" aspects of the job.
3. The psychological satisfaction you may, or may not, derive from the job.

It would be ridiculous to suggest any formulized approach to the problem of meeting the multiple targets in most job situations. The differences between specific jobs, specific companies, and most of all, between individuals, make such a formulation impossible. Still, there are some general observations that can be made regarding each of these targets and how you can best approach them.

First of all, you have to understand the mechanics of your particular job. It's the rare job that doesn't require some special skill, training, or educational background. Yet a great many people are surprisingly inept when it comes to the basic mechanics of their jobs. A high percentage of executives, for example, lack the basic writing skills needed to dictate a well-organized memorandum or business letter. Which means that a simple task—writing a letter—that should take only a few minutes ends up occupying an hour or two of an executive's time. I can understand a person not having basic writing skills. What's hard to understand is how few executives ever take any steps to improve these skills.

In this respect we can all use professional athletes as models. Professional athletes don't take their skills for granted. They keep in shape. They drill. They practice. They—the better ones, at least—are constantly working to improve their weaknesses. Athletes, in particular, appreciate the importance of fundamental skills in overall performance.

Each of us, regardless of what we do for a living, needs to develop an appreciation of the basic skills and the basic knowledge needed if we are to do what we do well. Developing these skills and expanding this knowledge should always be a target of whatever job situation we happen to be in.

The second target mentioned above—social and political aspects of your job—affects some of us more than others. Some companies or organizations are more "political" than others. Some professions require more in the way of social interaction than others. And while we may not want to face up to it, it's hard to ignore this target. I know an excellent surgeon whose career has suffered because he has refused to seek admission into the various surgical societies. He keeps insisting he isn't interested in the politics of his profession—a noble point of view, but, at the same time, he's unhappy about his present hospital position.

"Office politics" is a fact of life in most professions, although people who overtarget in this area at the expense of job performance usually don't get very far. Indeed, attaching too much importance to the purely political aspects of your job is a common form of *misdirected targeting*. Still, whether or not you choose to address yourself to the targets that fall into this category is your affair, but you owe it to yourself to at least *recognize* the reality of your situation. If you work for a company rife with office politics and you aren't a political animal, you probably don't belong in that company. I'm making no value judgments here. It's simply a matter of recognizing a situation for what it is, and facing up to it.

Which brings us to the third target: the level of satisfaction you derive from your job. If there is one target many people seem to ignore more than any other, it's this one. It's impossible to estimate the number of "successful" people I've come to know who are desperately unhappy because they were so obsessed by their need to achieve, impress their superiors, and move up the ladder that they never stopped to think about whether or not they were deriving any real personal satisfaction from their work.

In work, as in many areas of life, there must be a balance. If you are performing tasks in your job that you find unpleasant and that you don't believe in, you're ignoring what should be a basic target: a job that you enjoy and take pride in. Even if you are successful in handling the mechanics of the job and in managing the political end of it, you will not be able to derive any real satisfaction from it.

Specific Job Targeting Skills

Certain jobs require a specific kind of target awareness. If you are in any sort of a supervisory position, you have to be concerned with not only your own targeting patterns but those of the people working under you as well. A common failing among supervisors is to assume that everyone who works under them shares the same basic targets. They usually don't. Some of your subordinates may only be interested in holding onto their jobs. Other people who work for you may be very ambitious and will need another kind of attention. Still others may work mainly for the satisfaction of doing a good job. By taking the time to get to know the people who work with you—and, in particular, getting a fix on what *their* targets are, you develop the sensitivity you need to become an effective leader.

Knowing, for instance, that a person working under you takes his job extremely seriously—this person's chief target, in other words, is to "do a good job"—might induce you to give him or her a specific assignment that you would not give someone else whose chief target is being political so as to advance up the corporate ladder. Knowing that a person takes pride in his or her job will help you adopt a supervisory strategy that might be different were you dealing with a person who is simply working "for the money."

Some years ago, there was a fine movie called *The Loneliness of the Long Distance Runner,* in which the head of a boys reformatory school in England made a false assumption about one of his charges. He had automatically assumed that the young inmate running in a long-distance race shared his own desire for a victory in a competition with a local school. When the young man stops only yards away from the finish line, the headmaster is shocked. The young runner was not at all concerned about a victory for the school; he ran because it gave him pleasure.

Similar rude awakenings are experienced almost daily by corporate executives who can't understand why some of the people under them don't share the same overall goals as they, the supervisors, do. Don't make the same mistake. Be sensitive to the targets of those around you as well. The more you appreciate the targets that energize the people you're trying to motivate, the more ammunition you have to motivate these people in the direction you want them to go.

Target Mutuality and Marriage

Few targets are more basic or more important to the average person than having a happy marriage. But it's obvious from the soaring divorce rate that this target is eluding more people than ever before.

By its very nature marriage must produce changes in individual targeting patterns. Once you are married, you can no longer continue to think exclusively in terms of your individual targets. Mutual targets become more important. Often it's an inability to adjust to these target changes that accounts for a high percentage of unhappy marriages.

The problems in this respect vary enormously. Some men find that while marriage satisfies their physical need for sex, it doesn't fill the psychological need that sexual conquest filled when they were single. Some women—and men, too—find it difficult to find in marriage the feedback that fills the psychological need to be admired and sought after.

Men and women in these categories deal with their situa-

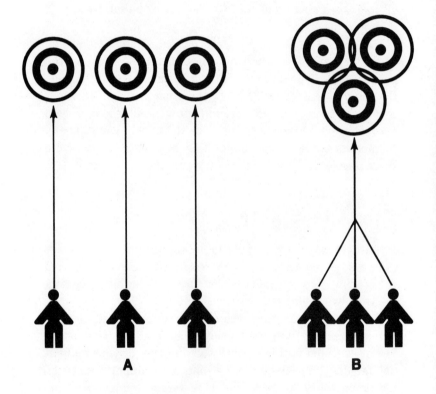

Target mutuality is the merging of the interests of several people with differing targets (*A*) by finding the common elements of the targets and bringing them into convergence (*B*). The process involves making people sensitive to the concerns and goals of others, and showing them that this does not necessarily conflict with their own interests.

tions in different ways. Some people sublimate unfulfilled psychosexual needs for success into their careers or into sports. Many who lack these sublimation outlets can become philanderers—some of them manage to combine extramarital activities with a satisfactory marriage, but others are clumsily unsuccessful at this admittedly difficult combination. Still others may become unreasonably tyrannical and demanding in the marriage, determined, in effect, to "make the wife pay" or "make the husband pay" for the "sacrifice" the spouse has been forced to make.

Some of these problems can be resolved in a much healthier manner. If a couple develops a solid and loving relationship, this nurturance is usually enough to reduce, if not eliminate, the needs that were previously met through sexual conquest. This doesn't mean that a person's sexual desire for partners other than his wife automatically disappears as soon as the marriage knot is tied. It means instead that what was once a *major* target has now become only a *minor* target. And as long as an individual is growing in other areas of his or her life, this target is likely to remain a minor target.

It's important to stress here that when a target has once occupied a very important position in your life (as in the case of a man whose sexual activities were high priority) it's unlikely that this target will ever completely disappear. It's not unusual for a man who has been a faithful husband for ten years or even more to find himself, at the age of thirty-five or so, upsettingly preoccupied with thoughts of extramarital sex. What usually happens is that the husband, for any number of reasons, has suddenly developed a need for sexual psychological reassurance. He is, in fact, usually going through a midlife crisis about himself, his goals, his possibilities. He may then revert to earlier targets, look for consolation in the source that provided it before.

I am making no moral judgments here. I've had patients who were quite satisfied with their marriage and family life, but nevertheless felt a strong desire for extramarital sexual adventure. In such cases I've tried to help such men understand that what is lacking in their lives is not so much an absence of sexual adventure (although frequently the problem has centered on their dissatisfaction with the sex in their marriages) but rather a more general feeling of lack of fulfillment. The danger in this kind of a situation is that a man can become so blinded by the reemergence of an earlier target (in this case sexual adventure) that he'll take steps and make decisions undermining many of the more fundamental targets that have long occupied an important part in his life.

Targeting analysis helps us gain better insight into another common marriage pattern: that of women who have been encouraged to see marriage as a target complete and of itself, never thinking beyond it. This view has faded somewhat recently, due to the increasing career possibilities for women, but there are, nevertheless, many women who still think of marriage as *the* goal, the one solution to their lives. Two types of problems tend to emerge in such a situation.

In the first place, a woman whose chief target during her unmarried life is simply to become a "married woman" is quite likely to wind up with a man she wouldn't normally choose were her need to be married not quite as desperate. Marriage, in and of itself, is not a healthy target to pursue, and a woman whose desire for marriage clouds her ability to judge the man she is marrying will cheat herself. Any satisfaction she feels upon achieving her target will usually be short-lived and will often be followed by years of unhappiness and frustration, generally relieved only by divorce.

But even if a woman is fortunate enough to marry a congenial suitable man, it's unrealistic for her to assume that marriage alone—or even motherhood—will be enough of a target to satisfy the needs she may develop to be an independent person.

Today, of course, many women are taking a much harder

look at themselves, and discovering that their needs are not being met by the present quality of their lives.

Too many women, though, think only in terms of negative targets: "I don't like being tied down," or, "I don't want to be just a housewife or a mother any longer." Such sentiments are extremely understandable, but it is far more effective for one to formulate *positive* targets than negative ones. Positive targets are more easily integrated into the framework of an existing life. For example, after declaring that your life is empty and unfulfilled, it is natural, practical, and sensible as a second step to ask, "What can be done to change it?" But the danger here is an answer of "I don't know," which closes all doors to discovery. If on the other hand you begin by saying, "Let me find out what I can do to make things better," your mind may be more open to alternatives.

MAKING MARRIAGE WORK

If there is one thing I've learned as a psychiatrist, it is that there is no set formula for a successful marriage. I've seen successful marriages in which the husband and wife appeared to have almost nothing in common. I've seen terrible marriages in which the couple appeared to have everything in common. I've known couples who were highly compatible with one another sexually yet couldn't begin to satisfy each other's *non*sexual needs. I've also known couples whose marriages have worked out well even though their sex life together was a very minor and inconsequential part of the marriage. The point is, nobody outside a marriage can accurately see what it is that makes one marriage "work" and one marriage "fail."

But if I had to name the one factor that more than any other contributes to a good marriage, I would say it was "consideration"—of another's needs and desires. To put it in targeting terms, it is a well-developed sensitivity toward the spouse's targets. The absence of this sensitivity and consideration is what I have found most often in failing or failed marriages.

All too often, a couple after several years gets accustomed to living together and a certain insensitivity develops. Long-married couples frequently begin to take one another for granted. The husband, for instance, begins to assume that his principal responsibility in the marriage is to be a good provider and a loving father to his children. Pressured in his job, he sees his home as a sanctuary—a place where he can come to rest and relax, and where he need not worry about satisfying the needs of his wife.

In some marriages this attitude doesn't cause serious problems, for the wife may not demand much more than his economic support. But if the wife has no real life outside the marriage and the husband gives little thought or energy to her feelings, his attitude can be a source of constant unhappiness to her.

What is curious about marriages in which the couples are not sensitive to the needs of one another is that very frequently it doesn't require much effort on either side to ease the troublesome situation. I can think of one strained marriage that underwent an incredible transformation once the husband made it a point, when he got home, not to go for the evening paper or to read the mail, but simply to sit down and chat with his wife for ten minutes. That's all, just ten minutes a day, but it made all the difference.

Helping men and women become more sensitive to one another's needs is one of the things that marriage counselors try to do with couples experiencing marital problems. Sex is a common area of difficulty—more so today than ever before, now that women are becoming less inhibited about recognizing and voicing their own sexual needs and desires. Until recently women have been obliged to subordinate their sexual appetites to the convenience and whims of their husbands.

Unfortunately, women who have liberated themselves from old-fashioned inhibitions may often put more pressure, knowingly or unknowingly, on the husband than he can deal with. Once again, we're back to the fundamental ingredient in a happy marriage: a mutuality of targets.

TARGETING AND PARENTHOOD

Still another crucial area of interpersonal relations is parenting. Here, too, targeting has a useful application. Apart from providing enough love, understanding, and guidance, effective parenting (in targeting terms) really comes down to achieving a happy balance between the targets you set for your children and the targets they themselves establish throughout the course of their development. The problem, though, is that parents and children frequently find themselves face to face with legitimate targets that are in conflict. A typical conflict occurs when a child wants to do something that the parent feels is dangerous or inappropriate. In this case, the common parental target of "wanting to make the child happy" conflicts with the parental target of "looking out for the child's safety."

There is no easy solution to such a conflict. The best thing that can be said is that in most cases as a parent you have a pretty good margin of error. I do not advocate either an overly strict or an overly permissive approach to parenting. There must be balance. Constantly thwarting the *reasonable* wishes of a child will create frustration and inhibit a child's intellectual curiosity. Then again, it's impossible to abolish the word "no" entirely when you're raising a child. Some frustration is good for a child. It forces him or her to adjust behavior according to the demands of a situation. What should be avoided, though, are situations in which frustration becomes the dominant force in the child's life.

As a child grows older, the potential for parental conflicts tends to get more intense—particularly when the parents exert a great deal of pressure on the child to move in a particular direction toward a particular target. This brings us to one of the greatest traps of being a parent: confusing our own ends with the targets we set for our children. There are frequently situations in which the child genuinely wants to pursue the same target as the parent. But even in these cases a child will often resist any amount of pressure to move in a particular direction—not because he doesn't want to necessarily move in that direction, but because he wants to make his own decisions.

Sometimes our own missed achievements and targets are imposed on our children. I remember one family in which the father wanted to become a professional football player. He didn't quite make it, and years later was determined that his son, who was a very gifted athlete in high school, would succeed where he himself had failed. The father placed a great amount of pressure on his son. Soon the boy started to suffer a remarkable succession of injuries. First he broke a finger. Then he developed a bad knee. Then he suffered a series of fractures. Kids who play contact sports are certainly prone to injuries, but in this case the injuries seemed excessive. It became fairly obvious that getting hurt was the boy's way of avoiding the pressure being put on him by his father.

I remember another instance of a father who desperately wanted his son to be a lawyer. He came to see me because his son—a straight A student in college—had been caught cheating on an exam. The son eventually did go to law school and graduate, but a year or so after he went to work for a law firm, the son decided he really didn't want to be a lawyer. The sad part about this situation is that the father never could accept his son's decision and it just about destroyed their relationship.

Would the son in this situation have remained a lawyer if it had not been for the fierce pressure his father had kept on him? It's hard to say. My guess is that without the pressure the boy probably wouldn't have gone to law school, but at least the relationship between the father and the son wouldn't have been destroyed.

I'm not suggesting that it's wrong for a parent to have targets for his children. A parent's role includes that of counselor and a parent must help point the child in life. The danger arises when forcing a child to reach a target becomes the target in and of itself. As parents, we all have to recognize—and it's not always easy—that the older our children get the greater becomes their need to think for themselves and choose for themselves. With certain children, the development of attitudes and the adopting of a life-style running counter to what the parents might want is less an affirmation of these opposing attitudes and life-style than it is in fact a rejection of parental pressures. Not long ago I saw a woman patient who was having a terrible conflict with her fifteen-year-old daughter over the boy her daughter was going out with. From what the woman told me, she had every right to be upset about the romance, but the more she complained about the boy to her daughter and the more she kept reminding her daughter about the boy's bad qualities, the more she forced her daughter into a defensive posture. Without knowing it, the woman was actually reinforcing her daughter's love affair, not achieving her target of breaking it up.

There are no hard and fast rules about bringing up children, but by learning to recognize the need that children have to make their own decisions and go their own way, by recognizing that what *we* would like for our children may not necessarily be what will most benefit them we can, at least, keep open the lines of communication, without which a loving and warm parent/child relationship is impossible.

TARGET PRACTICE 11

Testing Your Target Orientation

Most people who work have as one of their prime targets the desire to "get ahead." But as we saw in this past chapter, job success calls for multiple targeting. The idea behind the following test is to give you a basic sense of how target-oriented you are in your present job and whether your current course of action is consistent with your overall career targets. To take the test, simply choose the answer that most accurately describes your particular situation.

1. **If I were asked to name the four most important aspects of my job or career, I could do it:**
   a. Easily
   b. With only a little bit of trouble
   c. With some difficulty
   d. With a good deal of difficulty
2. **I look forward to going to work:**
   a. Almost always
   b. Usually
   c. Sometimes
   d. Hardly ever
3. **My job is well-suited to my skills:**
   a. Definitely
   b. Pretty much so
   c. Somewhat
   d. Not at all
4. **I get bored at work:**
   a. Hardly ever
   b. Occasionally
   c. Much of the time
   d. Nearly always

5. If I had to do it over again, I would choose my present line of work:
   a. Certainly
   b. Probably
   c. Probably not
   d. Definitely not

6. I envy the jobs and careers that many of my friends are pursuing:
   a. Not at all
   b. Somewhat
   c. Pretty much so
   d. Very much so

7. I'm satisfied with the progress I'm making in my career:
   a. Very much so
   b. Pretty much so
   c. Not too much
   d. Not at all

8. I feel as if I'm "over my head" in my job:
   a. Hardly ever
   b. Occasionally
   c. Much of the time
   d. Nearly always

9. I know what I have to do in order to move ahead in my job:
   a. Very much so
   b. Pretty much so
   c. Not really
   d. Not at all.

10. There are several jobs and positions above me in my job or profession that I can easily see myself moving into in the future:
    a. Very much so
    b. Pretty much so
    c. Not really
    d. Not at all

Scoring

Give yourself 4 points for every (a) answer; 3 points for every (b) answer; 2 points for every (c) answer; and 1 point for every (d) answer.

34 to 40. If you scored 34 or better in this test, chances are you're on the right career track. You like what you do, and you have a clear idea of what you have to do to get ahead, and you're optimistic about your future.

28 to 33. A score of between 28 and 33 indicates that, by and large, you're doing what you want to do and are probably well-suited for the work. Still, there are some aspects of your work in which a more target-oriented approach could yield some benefits. Take a special look at any area in which you answered (c) or (d).

20 to 27. A score on this level shows fairly clearly that you're not deriving either the satisfaction or the results from your job or career that you want to derive. Try to see where your problem areas are—in the mechanics of the job itself or in your relation to the work. If you're good at your job but still scored between 20 and 27, chances are you're not in a field that's best suited to your temperament and aspirations. It may be time to think in terms of a change. If you like your job very much but still didn't score above 27, you'd do well to take a close, hard look at what your job entails and what you have to do to get better at it.

19 or below. A score of 19 or below is a reasonably reliable indication that you are in a job for which you are not well-suited and from which you derive little satisfaction. Then again, you probably don't need to be told this. It's time to take some positive action.

CHAPTER 12

Making It Work

Few people appreciate more than psychiatrists the pitfalls inherent in giving advice on how to live a happier and more successful life, and this danger has been foremost in my mind throughout this book. As I mentioned early on, targeting is not a guaranteed formula for happiness—or even a prescription for success in the various areas of your life. The basic idea behind it is to give you more control over the one element that more than any other will determine what you accomplish in life and how much satisfaction you derive from this accomplishment: you yourself.

At its root, targeting involves nothing more than having a clear idea of what it is you want to accomplish in each of the various areas and activities that make up your life on a day to day basis. This is why I've worked so hard to make a distinction throughout this book between behavior that is target oriented and behavior that is aimless. The fact that your behavior is target oriented is no guarantee, of course, that it will bring about the results you desire, anymore than taking aim at an archery target is a guarantee that you'll hit a bull's-eye. Then again, it hardly needs reemphasizing that aimless behavior is, by definition almost, behavior that stands little chance of producing the kind of results that will provide you with the sense of self-esteem that has proved itself to be so elusive to so many people in this age of psychological confusion.

I recognize that I've made a number of points in this book and offered a number of suggestions that may not have relevance to your particular life situation. But as I've said at different times throughout the book, targeting is not a rigid, formulized approach to living but rather a general concept made up of many simple concepts, any one of which may be useful to you in a variety of ways. You have to experiment with many of these techniques, in some cases making minor modifications to meet your particular targeting needs. Indeed, it's possible that by now you've come up with several targeting techniques of your own.

So rather than close out *Targets* with a summary of the specific techniques mentioned and explained in earlier chapters, let me summarize for you a few of the main overall targeting principles that underlie these techniques. By keeping these overall principles in mind and by gaining an appreciation of what they contribute to your life, you should be able to incorporate targeting into your life in ways that will not only make you a more productive and more organized person, but will enhance the pleasure and excitement you derive from the life process.

1. Developing Target Awareness

Never forget that behind virtually everything you do, large or small, major or minor, there is a purpose—whether you recognize it or not. So developing target awareness is nothing more than learning to recognize something that's already there: noticing the elephant that is right before your eyes. The simple question "What is my target?" is a question you can never ask yourself too often. Once you get into the habit of asking yourself this question whenever the situation demands it, you should find that the pointlessness and aimlessness of some actions you might normally take in a situation will become immediately apparent. You will realize, for example, that chewing out•one of your subordinates or scolding one of your children may serve to release some pent-up anger, but will do little to affect the conditions that led to the anger in the first place. You will also realize that the confusion that frequently surrounds the making of an important decision clears up considerably once you have a clear idea of what your objective is and how your options relate to that objective. You begin to think less in terms of what should I do, and more in terms of what needs to be done in order to achieve a certain set of objectives. You develop, in short, an approach to life that is more firmly rooted in the way things are, and not in the way you'd prefer them to be.

2. Recognizing the Hierarchy of Targets

As your sense of target awareness grows, so will your skill at recognizing the hierarchy of smaller targets that make up the major targets you set for yourself. You'll begin to see that the process everybody refers to as "planning" is really nothing more than establishing targets in a logical sequence. Thus, instead of attacking various tasks in a random fashion, you'll begin to sequence activities in a way that will help to eliminate the common problem of redundant effort. You'll be able to accomplish more in less time and with less effort—but without the need of applying additional skills or knowledge.

3. Organizing Your Time More Efficiently

The ability to sequence your targets more intelligently should enable you to establish a schedule for yourself that utilizes time not only in the most efficient manner but in a manner that produces the sense of balance so necessary to a satisfying life. A schedule, you'll begin to appreciate more and more, is not a straitjacket but rather a means of organizing your time in an intelligent manner suited to your particular situation. Here again you should see that simply by altering the order in which you pursue certain targets, you can accomplish more with the same amount of effort and, just as importantly, be able to enjoy to its fullest the time you set aside for leisure.

4. Digging In and Sticking With It

No matter what you do, you will occasionally find yourself unable to focus on targets that need to be attended to, or else bogged down on projects without knowing quite why. The reason for these problems can vary so much from person to person and from situation to situation that it's impossible to recommend any one sure-fire cure, but several of the techniques discussed throughout the book—target sweetening, positive side-tracking, etc.—can often get you started or put you back on the track without subjecting you to excessive frustration. Remember, though, these techniques and tricks are not the essence of targeting, they are merely tools to be used now and then, when the situation calls for them. If you run into these problems frequently, chances are there is something amiss in your basic approach to the things in life you want to accomplish.

5. Keeping Tabs

Nothing will sabotage a target-oriented approach to life more than the failure to maintain a running *written* account of the targets you establish and the success with which you reach these targets. If you've never consciously targeted before, you should start out by writing out targets on an almost daily basis, always referring to your basic list later in the day to keep track of your progress. After a couple of weeks of daily target tracking, you can do it on a less frequent basis—once or twice a week, say. Particularly important are the target-inventory techniques covered in Chapter 10. Even if you use none of the techniques mentioned throughout the book, the simple act of setting aside an hour or so every now and then to get a sense of where you are in relation to where you want to be in your job, your social relationships, your intellectual growth, etc., will establish an overall framework that in and of itself will give direction and focus to your life.

Bibliography

Burns, Robert C., and S. Kaufman, M.D., *Actions, Styles and Symbols in Family Drawings: An Interpretive Manual*. New York, Brunner/Mazel, 1972.

Darling, Lois and Louis, *A Place in the Sun: Ecology and the Living World*. New York, William Morrow, 1968.

Ekman, Paul, and Wallace Friesen, *Unmasking the Face*. Englewood Cliffs, N.J., Prentice-Hall, 1975.

Greenwald, Harold, ed., *Active Psychotherapy*. New York, Jason Aronson, 1974.

Kipling, Rudyard, *If*. New York, Doubleday.

Korda, Michael, *Success*. New York, Random House, 1977.

Masserman, Jules, and John Schwab, *Social Psychiatry*, Vol. I, New York, Grune & Stratton, 1974.

Mayeroff, Milton, *On Caring*. World Perspectives Series, edited by Ruth Nanda Anshen. New York, Harper & Row, 1971.

Tec, Leon, M.D., *Fear of Success*. New York, Readers Digest Press, 1976.

Watzlawick, Paul, *The Language of Change: Elements of Therapeutic Communication*. New York, Basic Books, 1978.

Index

191